LARD

The Lost Art of Cooking with Your Grandmother's Secret Ingredient

100% NATURAL

LARD

Editors of GRIT Magazine

Photography by
Thomas Gibson

Andrews McMeel
Publishing, LLC

Kansas City • Sydney • London

Andrews McMeel Publishing, LLC
an Andrews McMeel Universal company
1130 Walnut Street, Kansas City, Missouri 64106
www.andrewsmcmeel.com

12 13 14 15 16 RR2 10 9 8 7 6 5 4 3 2 1

ISBN: 978-1-4494-0974-6

Library of Congress Control Number: 2011932650

www.grit.com

www.LardCookbook.com

Design: Diane Marsh
Photography: Thomas Gibson
Food Stylist: Andrea Krakaw
Prop Stylist: Kate Dixon
Art Director: Tim Lynch
Contributing Editor: Karen Keb (photos pp. xii, 61)

ATTENTION: SCHOOLS AND BUSINESSES

Andrews McMeel books are available at quantity discounts with bulk purchase for educational, business, or sales promotional use. For information, please e-mail the Andrews McMeel Special Sales Department: specialsales@amuniversal.com

Contents

ACKNOWLEDGEMENTS

This project bubbled up during one of those delightfully stimulating brainstorming sessions in which our fearless leader, publisher, and friend, Bryan Welch, suggested we do something to combat the nearly century-long erosion of wholesome and healthful ingredients from pantries nationwide. Bryan (who farms in addition to running Ogden Publications) is an inspiration, and without his enthusiastic support, this project would have never gotten off the ground.

Lard is a tribute to the thousands of *GRIT* and *CAPPER's* readers who've contributed recipes to our extensive database for 130-plus years. This celebration of generations of grandmothers' secret ingredient is for you. Without your creative passion and generous sharing of techniques, this cookbook would not be possible.

Many thanks to Traci Smith, Jean Teller, and generations of other food editors for their care in maintaining our recipe database—Jean and Traci cheerfully applied their intuition and culinary knowledge to effectively sift through recipes untold, while bringing you the best of the best dishes that use lard as an ingredient. Thanks to Kathryn Compton for lending a bit of levity to the text.

With so many cooks, the *Lard* kitchen felt crowded at times. We appreciate the efforts of the dynamic duo Andrew and Laura Perkins, who, along with coworker Sherry Nusbaum, managed the compilation and editing process for us and handled the nitty-gritty interface with our publisher, Andrews McMeel. We're quite sure that this project would have fallen through the cracks had it not been for your gentle urging and commiseration over ever-looming deadlines. Thanks also for bringing Karen Keb onboard. Without her editing skills, food knowledge, and attention to detail, we would still be standardizing the recipe language.

We are grateful that the cookbook team at Andrews McMeel was willing to take a chance on this project. Thanks especially to Jean Lucas for her stern, precise, and professional guidance. I'm sure we seemed like the unruly child at times, but we so appreciate your insight and considerable efforts to turn *Lard* into the gem it is.

And finally, thanks to you, dear reader, for your undying interest in real food created with real, whole ingredients. Without you, this book would have no meaning.

GRIT editorial team

Even Our Publisher Loves Lard

When I was a boy, my grandparents' best friends were Roman and Eva Mendez. They lived about half a mile from us, over one sand hill in the tiny village of Anapra, New Mexico. We visited them once a week or so, and usually sat around for an hour or two, in the manner of that time, just to drink soft drinks and enjoy each other's company. It was a little disorienting because Roman and my grandfather spoke Spanish—Roman with a strong Chihuahuan accent and my grandfather in a kind of Oklahoma version of border Spanglish. Meanwhile, my grandmother and Eva spoke English, of a sort, in a lively uninterruptable chatter. It was hard for me to follow either conversation with any precision.

I tagged along for the tortillas.

Eva Mendez had a way with tortillas. Even in a culture that revered this traditional flatbread, Eva's tortillas were a revelation, a monument, a tribute to everything that alkaline water and white flour can become.

Oh, yeah. Alkaline water, white flour, and the irreplaceable lard.

A lot of families already were using canned shortening, but not Eva. Her tortillas were made with lard, and they were delicious. I didn't want butter on them. I didn't want honey. The unleavened white bread, warm from the skillet, was more tantalizing than any cookie, candy, or cake. It was, simply, better than anything.

Surely there was skill involved in making a tortilla that good. I haven't had another like it in my life. But there was also a secret ingredient: lard, pure and simple.

Bryan Welch, Grit publisher
Topeka, Kansas

Introduction

The LINGERING LEGACY of LARD

By Oscar H. Will III
Editor in Chief of GRIT and CAPPER's Magazines

Pig fat has been used for centuries in processes ranging from lubrication, lighting, cooking, soap making, and just plain eating. Lard-based oils and greases were an important component of machinery and engine lubrication until some years after the dawn of the petroleum age. The first oil wells were drilled with machinery lubricated with lard. Even into the 1930s, hog farmers could earn more from the lard an animal might produce than from the meat and by-products.

The first documented use of lard as food dates to the 1400s, and the healthful fat was big business three hundred years later. So big was the lard industry that hogs were bred specifically for that purpose—the meat was secondary to the fat. Historically, lard has been used in place of butter as a spread on breads and other starches; because of its properties as an excellent shortening, it remains prized by pastry chefs even today. Lard is an excellent cooking fat because it burns at a very high temperature and tends not to smoke as heavily as many other fats and oils.

Although it might seem to contradict conventional wisdom, we believe lard still has a place on your pantry shelf—and some of the best-tasting pies depend on it. As it turns out, many of the negative health claims ascribed to lard—and other animal fats— appear to have been largely exaggerated.

We humans crave the concentrated calories of animal fats. We are drawn to the aroma of foods fried in tallow (rendered beef fat) because animal fats have been a natural part of the human diet since the beginning. Consider that although those french fries you savor today have been fried in fats derived from plants, the folks doing the frying also added tallow flavor to the oil because the scent of foods fried in tallow is nearly impossible to resist.

In the United States, fats—animal fats in particular—have been vilified over the past century as we've struggled with our collective health, particularly arterial health, and our collective weight. The somewhat naive notion that fat consumed equals fat gained spread like wildfire, and when discoveries were made that linked certain kinds of fats with cholesterol and coronary artery diseases, the corn industry was ready to move in with a highly processed magic bullet—oleo, the perfect and "healthy" substitute for butter. Oleo now is often used synonymously with margarine, but margarine once contained animal fats such as lard. Delicious and nutritious animal fats such as lard were also replaced with a "healthy" and pure "vegetable shortening" that was pretty much guaranteed to keep Betty Crocker's figure intact while preventing heart disease among the masses.

When the switch to "healthy" plant-derived fats failed to keep the weight off the American public, we went looking for other magic bullets. Thus was born the "fat-free" revolution. Once again, we substituted highly processed fat-free foods for the real deal. The result is that we gained even more weight than the Health Department thought possible. In retrospect there's little surprise in that result. It has to do with the fundamental nature of consuming fats, as well as the fact that today we expend less physical energy in an average day than we did many decades ago.

Turns out that consuming fats helps you feel full and satisfied. Low-fat foods and most foods high in processed carbohydrates are not as effective at communicating with the brain to signal that you are full. Result: You eat more as you try to feel satisfied, and your weight climbs. Further, scientific studies show that elevated serum triglyceride levels are largely the result of your liver processing sugar, not fat. And since high serum triglycerides relate to heart and arterial disease, replacing fat with sugar wasn't a smart idea at all.

We've also been told to replace all saturated (hydrogenated) fats with unsaturated fats, but unless they are cold-pressed, many vegetable oils are heated and otherwise processed in the act of extracting them. To add insult to injury, many of the vegetable oils that wind up in processed foods are subjected to a chemical modification that partially saturates them to make them solid at room temperature, and many of those processes create *trans fats*, as opposed to the naturally occurring *cis fats*, terms that refer to fat's somewhat complicated chemistry. Scientists report that only about one-fourth of the fat found in disease-causing arterial blockages is saturated, while half the total fat found in those blockages was polyunsaturated.

Numerous scientific studies now point the finger of guilt at processed *trans fats* for contributing to cases of cancer and heart disease more than virtually any naturally occurring healthful fats. Related studies also indicate that certain kinds of animal fats known as omega-3 and omega-6 fats are actually essential to the diet—our brains and cells need those fats, but our bodies cannot make them from scratch.

Rediscovered in the 1990s, along with other healthful animal fats, lard is once again embraced by chefs and enlightened health-care professionals and dieticians. Pure unprocessed lard contains roughly 40 percent saturated fats and 45 percent monounsaturated fats. It's interesting to note that lard contains much less saturated fat than butter (54 percent) and a number of plant-derived fats. But not all lard is equal. Most of the lard available at the grocery store is a by-product of the "other white meat," lean pig, bred to meet demand when pork took the fall. In order to make this lard palatable, it undergoes such processing, including deodorizing and bleaching, that it barely resembles the real thing—and is far from healthy. But thanks to heritage hog breeders and other committed members of the culinary community, high-quality unadulterated lard can still be found. (Check the availability of unadulterated artisanal lard at www.LardCookbook.com.) Either way, don't be afraid to bring a little lard back to the table. Your taste buds, and quite possibly your heart, will be glad you did.

Sourcing Pure Lard

The easiest method for obtaining pure lard may well be to render it yourself. You will need access to the best pig fat you can get—preferably the leaf fat deposited around the kidney area of the animal. But if you can't find the fat, or don't care to render, you can find high-quality lard online, at the farmers' market, and at specialty markets.

For resouces, see page 220, or for the most updated list, go to www. LardCookbook.com.

HOW to RENDER LARD

By Karen Keb

Creating edible lard from pig fat at home involves harvesting the leaf fat (deposited in the kidney area) and back fat from the hog, grinding or dicing it, and processing.

1. Preheat the oven to 225°F.

2. Fill a large roasting pan with the chopped fat.

3. Roast slowly for 30 minutes to 1 hour until the fat has melted and you have protein particles and connective tissue floating on top.

4. Skim off the solid particles and set them aside for the chickens.

5. Pour the liquid fat through a mesh colander lined with a double layer of cheesecloth.

6. Store in a glass canning jar in the refrigerator or freezer. It will keep for months.

Use the lard in place of oil when frying, in pastry such as pie crusts, sautéing vegetables, or roasting potatoes. You'll be delighted with the texture and flavor (or lack of pork flavor) that real lard—not the hydrogenated kind sold on supermarket shelves—provides.

Chapter 1

BREADS and BISCUITS

GRANDMA'S HOMEMADE BISCUITS

These biscuits are as authentic as they come, from a time when lard from the family's hog and milk from the backyard cow were common fare. The dough can be rolled and cut with a biscuit cutter or dropped from a wooden spoon. Make these for a big family supper, as biscuits are best when eaten fresh from the oven. **Makes 1 dozen**

⅓ cup plus 1 tablespoon lard, cold and coarsely chopped, plus more for greasing the pan

2½ cups all-purpose unbleached flour

3 teaspoons baking powder

½ teaspoon salt

1 cup milk

1 tablespoon salted butter, melted (optional)

Preheat the oven to 400°F. Grease a baking sheet with lard and set aside.

Place 2 cups of flour, the baking powder, and the salt in a large mixing bowl; whisk together. Using a pastry blender, work the lard into the flour mixture until it resembles coarse crumbs. Add the milk and stir.

On a sheet of wax paper, sprinkle the remaining ½ cup of flour. Turn the dough mixture onto the wax paper and knead for 5 minutes. Roll out the dough to a 1-inch thickness and cut with a biscuit cutter; alternatively, drop the dough using a large spoon and pat down onto the prepared baking sheet spaced 1 inch apart. For color, brush the biscuits with melted butter, if desired. Bake for 20 minutes, or until the tops are golden brown.

SKY-HIGH BISCUITS

These jumbo-sized biscuits are aptly named because the combination of working yeast, baking powder, baking soda, cream of tartar, and yogurt engages in a bubbling chemical reaction that fills the dough with carbon dioxide, causing them to rise "sky high." Make them when you have guests to impress or lots of hungry mouths to feed. Serve with butter, honey, or jam. **Makes 1 dozen**

½ cup lard, cold and coarsely chopped, plus more for greasing the pan

2¼ teaspoons active dry yeast

¼ cup warm water (105° to 115°F)

2½ cups all-purpose unbleached flour

2 tablespoons sugar

1 teaspoon baking powder

1 teaspoon salt

¾ teaspoon cream of tartar

1½ teaspoons baking soda

1 cup plain yogurt

Preheat the oven to 425°F. Grease a baking sheet with lard and set aside.

In a small bowl, dissolve the yeast in the warm water. Let stand until foamy, 5 to 10 minutes.

In a large bowl, mix together the flour, sugar, baking powder, salt, cream of tartar, and baking soda. Using a pastry blender or two knives, cut the lard into the flour mixture until coarse crumbs form.

Make a well in the center of the flour mixture; add the yogurt and yeast all at once. Toss with a fork until the dry ingredients are moistened. Do not overmix.

On a floured surface, roll the dough to a ¾-inch thickness using a floured rolling pin. Cut the biscuits using a floured 2½-inch round biscuit cutter. Gather the trimmings and repeat.

Place the biscuits 1 inch apart on the prepared baking sheet. Bake for 12 to 15 minutes, until puffed and golden. Leave the biscuits on the baking sheet and cool for 5 minutes on a wire rack. Serve warm.

CHEESE ROLL BISCUITS

These delicious little rolls are so much more than biscuits. Bread flour gives them a chewy texture and crisp crust, and the addition of cheese and buttermilk introduces extra protein and makes for a satisfying side dish or snack. Make them with Monterey Jack or cheddar cheese for a brunch or potluck. Makes 2 dozen

¼ cup lard, cold and coarsely chopped, plus more for greasing the pan

2½ cups bread flour

1 teaspoon salt

½ teaspoon baking soda

2 teaspoons baking powder

1 cup buttermilk

1 cup grated cheese of your choice

Preheat the oven to 375°F. Grease a baking sheet with lard and set aside.

Sift together the flour, salt, baking soda, and baking powder in a large bowl. Using a pastry blender, cut in the lard until you have a texture resembling coarse crumbs. Add the buttermilk and mix lightly with a fork.

Turn the dough out onto a lightly floured surface. Knead lightly and roll out to a ¼-inch thickness using a floured rolling pin. Sprinkle the cheese evenly over the dough and roll up (like a jelly roll). Cut into ¾-inch-thick slices. Place, cut side down, 1 inch apart on the prepared baking sheet and bake for 25 to 30 minutes, until puffed and golden.

FREEZER BISCUITS

The concept of freezer biscuits is a solid one—make biscuits one day, then eat them all month, for that's how long they'll keep. Just pop the number of frozen biscuits you desire into a hot oven, and you'll have crisp and flaky homemade biscuits in no time at all. Better yet, there are no leftovers that would turn soggy or go to waste. Makes 1 dozen

2 cups all-purpose unbleached flour

4 teaspoons baking powder

½ teaspoon cream of tartar

¼ teaspoon salt

2 tablespoons sugar

½ cup lard, cold and coarsely chopped

⅔ cup milk

1 egg, beaten

Butter and honey, for serving

In a large bowl, mix together the flour, baking powder, cream of tartar, salt, and sugar. Using a pastry blender or two knives, cut in the lard until it resembles coarse crumbs.

Beat together the milk and egg; add to the flour mixture and stir until a ball forms. Turn out the dough onto a lightly floured surface and knead gently for a few minutes.

Line a baking sheet with wax paper and set aside. Using a rolling pin, roll out the dough to a ¾-inch thickness and cut with a biscuit cutter. Place the biscuits on the prepared baking sheet and cover with plastic wrap. Freeze the biscuits until solid (about 6 hours), then transfer to a zip-top plastic bag. Freeze for up to 1 month.

To use: Preheat the oven to 425°F. Line a baking sheet with parchment paper and on it place the frozen biscuits 1 inch apart. Do not thaw before baking. Bake for 20 minutes, until puffed and golden brown. Serve warm with butter and honey.

PANDORA BREAD

What comes out of Pandora's box? The answer is "just about everything," thus the perfect name for this bread. The variety of fruit—pumpkin, apricots, dates, plus applesauce—ensures a wonderfully moist and dense loaf (each weighing about 2 pounds), and a delightfully crisp crust is achieved as a result of the lard. This bread smells like pumpkin pie as it bakes and will draw a crowd to the kitchen! Serve with butter and a drizzle of honey, or a selection of cheeses for a more substantial snack. Makes 2 loaves

⅔ cup lard, softened, plus more for greasing the pan

1¼ cups granulated sugar

1¼ cups brown sugar, packed

4 large eggs

1 cup applesauce

1 cup pureed pumpkin

2 cups all-purpose unbleached flour

1½ cups whole-wheat flour

2 teaspoons baking soda

½ teaspoon baking powder

½ teaspoon salt

½ teaspoon cinnamon

¼ teaspoon mace

¼ teaspoon nutmeg

¼ teaspoon cloves

⅔ cup chopped dried apricots

⅔ cup chopped pitted dates

1 cup chopped walnuts

Preheat the oven to 350°F. Grease two 9 by 5-inch loaf pans with lard and set aside.

In a large bowl, beat the lard and the sugars with an electric mixer on medium speed until well blended. Add the eggs, one at a time, and beat until thoroughly mixed. Beat in the applesauce and pumpkin.

In a separate bowl, stir together the flours, baking soda, baking powder, salt, and spices. Stir the flour mixture into the applesauce mixture, mixing just until the flour is moistened, then beat on low speed until well blended. Stir in the apricots, dates, and walnuts. Spoon the batter equally into the prepared pans.

Bake for 1 hour, or until a toothpick inserted in the center comes out clean and the bread just begins to pull away from the sides of the pan.

Let cool in the pans for 10 minutes, then turn the loaves out onto a wire rack. Serve warm or at room temperature. To store, wrap tightly with plastic and refrigerate for up to 1 week or freeze.

BEHIND THE TIMES Fresh homemade bread, spread with lard and sprinkled with sugar, makes a delicious sandwich. After remembering this from my childhood, I Googled "lard sandwich" and found that I am way behind the times. There were so many postings, I got lost in a netherworld of the "wonderful uses of lard."

Donald Brooks, Ringgold, Georgia

BUTTERMILK BREAD

Here's a classic sandwich bread you'll make over and over again. The buttermilk adds tang, and keeps the bread tender, light, and moist. Use one loaf while fresh, then slice and freeze the other for future use. If you're lucky enough to have access to fresh raw buttermilk, be sure to scald it (heat to just shy of boiling) in the first step since it contains an enzyme that interferes with yeast development; scalding is not necessary for pasteurized milk. Makes 2 loaves

1 cup buttermilk

3 tablespoons sugar

2⅓ teaspoons salt

⅓ cup lard, softened, plus more for greasing the bowl and pan

2¼ teaspoons active dry yeast

1 cup warm water

¼ teaspoon baking soda

5½ to 5¾ cups all-purpose unbleached flour

In a saucepan, slowly heat the buttermilk to simmering. Remove from the heat and allow to cool for 5 minutes. In a small bowl, combine the buttermilk, sugar, salt, and lard; set aside.

In a large mixing bowl, sprinkle the yeast over the warm water and stir until dissolved. Stir in the buttermilk mixture. Add the baking soda and 3 cups of flour; beat on medium-low speed until smooth. Mix in enough of the remaining flour to make a stiff dough.

Turn out the dough onto a lightly floured board and knead for 10 minutes, until it's smooth and elastic. Place the dough in a lightly greased bowl, turning once to coat, and cover with a towel. Let rise in a warm place for about 1 hour, or until doubled in bulk.

Grease two 9 by 5-inch loaf pans with lard. Cut the dough in half, shape into logs, and place in the prepared pans. Cover with plastic wrap and let rise in a warm place (70° to 78°F) for about 1 hour, until the dough peeks above the pan.

Preheat the oven to 400°F. Bake the loaves for 45 minutes until golden brown, or until an internal temperature of 195°F is reached. Remove from the oven and turn out onto a wire rack to cool completely.

LARD ON BREAD I was raised on farms, and I learned to cook and bake with lard. My pie crust was always flaky. My ex-mother-in-law asked me to show her how I made mine, though I had always thought her pies were delicious. She always lived on a ranch and cooked with lard.

I love lard spread on a slice of bread and seasoned with salt and black pepper.

I know this has nothing to do with cooking or baking, but we also used lard for hand cream, and it made our skin very soft.

Mary Nida Smith, Lakeview, Arkansas

BANANA BREAD

The addition of whole-wheat flour adds some heft and enhances the nutty taste of this classic quick bread. Be sure to use heavily speckled bananas (almost black) when making banana bread or the taste will be decidedly bland. Very ripe, heavily speckled bananas contain three times as much fructose (the sweetest sugar in fruit) than less spotty ones. Serve warm with butter, cream cheese, or even maple syrup.   Makes 1 loaf

½ cup lard, softened, plus more for greasing the pan

1½ cups self-rising flour

1 cup whole-wheat flour

½ teaspoon baking soda

1 teaspoon baking powder

¼ teaspoon salt

½ cup brown sugar, packed

2 eggs, beaten

1 teaspoon vanilla extract

1½ cups mashed bananas (3 to 4 extra-ripe medium bananas)

½ cup chopped pecans

Preheat the oven to 350°F. Grease a 9 by 5-inch loaf pan with lard and set aside.

In a large bowl, combine the flours, baking soda, baking powder, and salt; set aside.

In a separate large bowl, cream the lard with the brown sugar using a large rubber spatula until a thick paste is formed. Add the eggs and vanilla and mix well. Fold in the bananas and pecans. Add the flour mixture and stir until just moistened. Do not overmix.

Spoon the batter into the prepared pan and bake for 1 hour, until golden brown and a toothpick inserted in the center comes out clean. Cool on a wire rack.

INDIAN FRY BREAD

Fry bread is the Native American counterpart to Mexican tortillas. Thicker and more substantial than tortillas, fry bread is delicious and filling, and made with lard and dry milk, truly authentic, as Indians did not commonly have access to fresh milk. To substitute fresh milk in this recipe, use 2 to 2½ cups warmed milk and omit the water. Serve with a selection of taco fillings—seasoned meat, cheese, onions, lettuce, salsa, and beans—for a fun twist on "taco night."
Makes 1 dozen

4 cups all-purpose unbleached flour

1 heaping teaspoon baking powder

¾ cup instant dry milk

1 teaspoon salt

2 to 2½ cups warm water

Lard, for frying

In a large bowl, mix together the flour, baking powder, dry milk, and salt. Add the warm water and mix, using just enough to form a soft dough; cover and set aside for 2 to 3 hours.

Turn the dough onto a floured board and knead for 1 minute. Shape the dough into a log and cut into 12 even pieces. Using a rolling pin, roll out into 5-inch rounds.

Heat the lard to 360°F in a cast-iron skillet ½ inch deep. Fry the dough pieces, one at a time, for 1 to 2 minutes on each side until lightly browned. Drain and cool on paper towels.

CRANBERRY QUICK BREAD

Make this sweet-tart quick bread for brunch or midafternoon snacks. With quick breads, the key is to never overmix the batter; overmixing results in tough bread and muffins. Mix just enough to incorporate the flour but not so much that you end up with a smooth batter (craggy is good in this case). For best results, stir—don't beat. Makes 1 loaf

¼ cup melted lard, slightly cooled, plus more for greasing the pan

3 cups all-purpose unbleached flour

3 teaspoons baking powder

1½ teaspoons salt

1 cup sugar

1 cup fresh coarsely chopped cranberries

1 tablespoon grated orange or lemon zest

1 egg, slightly beaten

1½ cups milk

Preheat the oven to 350°F. Grease a 9 by 5-inch loaf pan with lard and set aside.

In a large bowl, sift together the flour, baking powder, salt, and ½ cup of sugar. In another bowl, mix the cranberries and zest with the remaining ½ cup of sugar; add to the dry ingredients and mix well.

In a separate bowl, combine the egg, milk, and lard; add to the cranberry mixture all at once, stirring just enough to moisten the dry ingredients. Spoon into the prepared loaf pan and bake for 1 hour, until golden brown and a toothpick inserted in the center comes out clean. Cool completely before slicing.

PINEAPPLE NUT LOAF

Reminiscent of pineapple upside-down cake, this quick bread is just as delicious when served for dessert, with a dollop of homemade vanilla ice cream or whipped cream alongside. We love the sweet and mild taste of pecans in this recipe, but whatever nuts you have in the pantry will do just fine. Makes 1 loaf

¼ cup lard, softened, plus more for greasing the pan

¾ cup brown sugar, packed

1 egg

2 cups all-purpose unbleached flour

1 teaspoon baking soda

½ teaspoon salt

½ (6-ounce) can frozen orange juice concentrate, thawed

1 cup crushed pineapple, undrained

½ cup chopped nuts of your choice

Preheat the oven to 350°F. Grease a 9 by 5-inch loaf pan with lard and set aside.

In a large bowl, cream together the brown sugar and lard with a hand mixer on low speed; add the egg and beat well.

In a separate bowl, stir together the flour, baking soda, and salt. Alternately add the dry ingredients and the orange juice concentrate to the brown sugar mixture, mixing well after each addition. Stir in the pineapple and nuts.

Spoon the mixture into the prepared pan and bake 50 to 60 minutes, until golden brown and a toothpick inserted in the center comes out clean. Cool completely before slicing.

SPANISH CORN BREAD

Plain old corn bread is a family favorite, but this spicy dressed-up version will delight and surprise them. Filled with chunks of corn and jalapeños, and topped with melted cheese, this side dish is almost a meal in itself. It's versatile enough to serve with a bowl of spicy chili on a cold day, or a crisp, veggie-filled garden salad on a hot one. For a bit of sweetness to temper the heat of the jalapeños, serve with honeyed butter. Makes 9 servings

½ cup lard, melted and cooled slightly, plus more for greasing the pan

1 cup finely ground cornmeal

1 teaspoon salt

1 teaspoon sugar

3 teaspoons baking powder

⅔ cup buttermilk

2 eggs

1 (8.5-ounce) can cream-style corn

1 (4-ounce) can chopped jalapeños

1 cup grated cheddar cheese

Preheat the oven to 350°F. Grease an 8 by 8-inch glass baking dish with lard and set aside.

Place the cornmeal, salt, sugar, and baking powder in a large bowl and whisk together. Add the buttermilk, eggs, lard, and corn and mix well (the batter will be thin).

Pour half the batter into the prepared baking dish. Distribute the jalapeños evenly over the batter and cover with half of the cheese. Pour the rest of the batter on top and sprinkle with the remaining cheese.

Bake for 30 minutes, until golden brown and a toothpick inserted in the center comes out clean. Cool for 10 minutes before slicing.

APPLESAUCE CIRCLE DOUGHNUTS

In the old days, doughnuts didn't carry the stigma they do today. Homemade with pure ingredients and fried in lard from the family's hog, they were a Sunday treat after church. Of course, one can't eat doughnuts every day, nor would we ever want to eat the store-bought variety because of their trans fats and preservatives. Treat your family to these delicious doughnuts that call to mind those apple cider doughnuts so popular at orchards in fall. Makes 3½ dozen

5 cups all-purpose unbleached flour

4 teaspoons baking powder

1 teaspoon baking soda

2 teaspoons salt

1 teaspoon nutmeg

1 teaspoon cinnamon

¼ teaspoon mace

¼ cup lard, softened, plus more for frying

1 cup granulated sugar

3 eggs

1 teaspoon vanilla extract

1 cup applesauce

½ cup buttermilk

GLAZE

2 cups confectioners' sugar

¼ cup apple cider

In a large bowl, sift together the flour, baking powder, baking soda, salt, and spices. Set aside.

In a separate large bowl, cream together the lard, granulated sugar, and eggs. Beat in the vanilla, applesauce, and buttermilk. Add the flour mixture, 1 cup at a time, beating until smooth after each addition. The dough will be tacky and moist—a cross between quick bread batter and cookie dough. Cover and chill for 1 hour.

Turn the dough onto a lightly floured board and roll out to a ⅜-inch thickness. Cut into pieces with a 2½-inch doughnut cutter.

In a cast-iron kettle, heat the lard to 2 inches deep and 350°F. Using a metal spatula, slide 3 to 4 doughnuts into the lard at a time and fry for 1 minute on each side, until golden brown all over. Remove from the fat with a slotted spoon and drain on paper towels. Bring the lard back to temperature between each batch.

To prepare the glaze, whisk together the confectioners' sugar and apple cider until smooth. After the doughnuts have cooled for 5 to 10 minutes, dip the tops in the glaze.

BAKED DOUGHNUTS

If you'd rather not deal with deep-fat frying, you don't have to forgo homemade doughnuts—try this baked version. An old-fashioned canvas pastry cloth and rolling pin cover will help you handle the sticky dough; none of the modern gadgets—such as ice-filled rolling pins or silicone mats—do a better job. To use these tools, just coat the cloth and stretchy rolling pin sleeve with flour and you're ready to go. The fabric prevents the dough from sticking by absorbing the excess flour.   Makes 2 dozen

4½ teaspoons active dry yeast

¼ cup warm water

1½ cups milk (heated, then cooled to lukewarm)

½ cup sugar, plus more for dusting

1 teaspoon salt

1 teaspoon nutmeg

¼ teaspoon cinnamon, plus more for dusting

2 eggs

⅓ cup lard, melted and cooled, plus more for greasing the pan

4½ cups all-purpose unbleached flour

¼ cup salted butter, melted

Dissolve the yeast in the warm water and let stand for 5 minutes.

Add the milk, sugar, salt, nutmeg, cinnamon, eggs, lard, and 2 cups of the flour. Beat with an electric mixer on low speed for 30 seconds, scraping the bowl constantly. Beat for 2 minutes at medium speed, scraping the bowl occasionally. Stir in the remaining 2½ cups of flour, scraping the sides of the bowl, until you have a smooth, elastic dough. Cover with plastic wrap and let rise in a warm place until the dough is doubled in size, 50 to 60 minutes.

Grease a baking sheet with lard and set aside.

Turn the dough onto a well-floured pastry cloth; roll it around lightly to coat with flour (the dough will be soft and tacky). With a floured, cloth-covered rolling pin, gently roll out the dough to a ½-inch thickness. Cut with a floured 2½-inch doughnut cutter. Lift the doughnuts carefully with a spatula and place 2 inches apart on the prepared baking sheet. Brush the doughnut tops with melted butter. Cover with plastic wrap and set in a warm spot to rise until doubled in size, about 20 minutes.

Preheat the oven to 425°F. Bake the doughnuts for 8 to 10 minutes, or until golden brown. Remove from the oven and immediately brush with the remaining melted butter; allow to cool for 1 to 2 minutes.

Place some sugar and a pinch of cinnamon in a paper bag; shake to combine. Place the cooled doughnuts, one at a time, inside the bag and shake to coat well.

DOUGHNUTS IN LARD

Call me stubborn, but I still fry my homemade doughnuts in lard. When our children were young, we raised pigs, and I would render the fat and use it for cooking. As the world changed, and we used less lard in regular cooking, I would still save it for doughnuts. The rest of the lard I would use to make soap.

My children raise pigs now, but they do not use the fat, so I have them save it for me, and I render it to make soap. I help with a mission in Uganda, and I use the lard to make soap to send over there. And I like it for myself, as well: Homemade soap lasts so much longer than store-bought soap.

I used to make biscuits with lard; they were snow white and very light. Now I make squash doughnuts, sour-milk doughnuts (my mother got the recipe from the *Grit* newspaper), and our favorite, raised glazed doughnuts. I only make them when the whole family is around, so we can enjoy them warm.

Jan Wood, Bremen, Maine

MASHED POTATO DOUGHNUTS

If you've got some leftover mashed potatoes, cake doughnuts are a delicious (and creative) way to use them up. Potatoes help baked goods retain moisture so you'll end up with light and fluffy, irresistibly tender doughnuts. You won't taste anything reminiscent of potatoes, but the starch adds a bit of richness. For a variation, substitute pureed pumpkin for the potatoes and roll the fried doughnuts in cinnamon sugar. Makes 5 dozen

6 cups all-purpose unbleached flour, sifted

7 teaspoons baking powder

1 teaspoon salt

1 teaspoon nutmeg

3 eggs

2 cups sugar, plus more for dusting

1½ cups mashed potatoes (with no added milk or butter)

6 tablespoons lard, melted, plus more for frying

¾ cup milk

In a large bowl, sift together the sifted flour, baking powder, salt, and nutmeg.

In a separate bowl, beat the eggs until the yolks and whites are mixed, then beat in the sugar, potatoes, and melted lard until well mixed. Stir in the milk. Add the dry ingredients, mixing just until all the flour is moistened (the dough will be tacky and moist). Cover with plastic wrap and chill for 1 hour or longer.

Turn the dough onto a lightly floured board and roll out to a ½-inch thickness. Cut the dough into pieces with a 2½-inch doughnut cutter.

In a cast-iron kettle, heat the lard to 1 inch deep and 350°F. Using a metal spatula, slide 3 to 4 doughnuts into the lard at a time and fry for 1 minute on each side, until golden brown all over. Remove from the lard with a slotted spoon and drain on paper towels. Bring the lard back to temperature between each batch.

Place some sugar on a large plate. When the doughnuts have cooled for 1 to 2 minutes, roll them in sugar and place on a serving plate.

SPICED CAKE DOUGHNUTS

The addition of cinnamon and nutmeg spices up these doughnuts, or try substituting other flavors such as cardamom or allspice. If you can get your hands on Snow White Non-Melting Sugar (sold online by King Arthur Flour), treat yourself. It won't melt or turn gummy and it makes for a long-lasting coating, though these doughnuts probably won't last long. **Makes 3 dozen**

3½ cups all-purpose unbleached flour

1 teaspoon salt

5 teaspoons baking powder

1 teaspoon cinnamon

½ teaspoon nutmeg

2 tablespoons lard, softened, plus more for frying

¾ cup granulated sugar

2 eggs

¾ cup milk

1 cup confectioners' sugar

In a large bowl, sift together the flour, salt, baking powder, cinnamon, and nutmeg. Set aside.

Cream the lard and granulated sugar together; add the eggs and milk, and beat on low speed. Add the flour mixture, 1 cup at a time, beating until smooth after each addition (the dough will be tacky and moist). Cover with plastic wrap and chill for at least 1 hour.

Turn the dough onto a lightly floured board and roll out to a ⅜-inch thickness. Cut the dough into pieces with a 2½-inch doughnut cutter; cover loosely with plastic wrap and let stand for 15 minutes.

In a cast-iron kettle, heat the lard to 1 inch deep and 375°F. Using a metal spatula, slide 3 to 4 doughnuts into the lard at a time and fry for 1 minute on each side, until golden brown all over. Remove from the lard with a slotted spoon and drain on paper towels. Bring the lard back to temperature between each batch.

Place the confectioners' sugar in a paper bag. Once the doughnuts have cooled for 1 to 2 minutes, place 1 doughnut at a time inside the bag; shake to coat well.

BERRY MUFFINS

When berries are in season and abundant, sometimes it's a chore to figure out something creative to make with them other than cobblers or crisps. Bake them up in these delicious breakfast muffins for something different. You can even substitute raspberries and blackberries—just choose firmer fruits for the latter and make sure to dry them well before stirring into the batter. Serve with fresh butter and preserves. **Makes 12**

¼ cup lard, softened, plus more for greasing the pan

2 cups all-purpose unbleached flour

1 tablespoon baking powder

½ teaspoon salt

¼ cup unsalted butter, softened

½ cup sugar

1 egg, beaten

1 cup milk

1 cup fresh blueberries, washed and dried

1 cup fresh strawberries, washed, dried, stemmed, and quartered

Preheat the oven to 400°F. Lightly grease 12 muffin cups with lard or line with paper baking cups; set aside.

In a medium bowl, sift the flour with the baking powder and salt; set aside.

In a large bowl, cream the butter with the lard and sugar; add the egg and beat on medium speed until light and fluffy. Alternately add the flour mixture and the milk to the lard mixture, stirring by hand after each addition until just moistened. Fold in the blueberries and strawberries. Do not overmix.

Spoon the batter into the prepared muffin cups, filling two-thirds full. Bake for 20 to 25 minutes, until golden and a toothpick inserted in the center of a muffin comes out clean. Cool completely before serving.

OATMEAL–RAISIN MUFFINS

If you like oatmeal–raisin cookies, you'll love these easy muffins. The turbinado sugar and cinnamon topping give these a streusel-like, crunchy bite. The oats and brown sugar contribute a palate-pleasing butterscotch flavor. Serve with butter and a drizzle of maple syrup. **Makes 12**

¼ **cup lard, cold and coarsely chopped, plus more for greasing the pan**

1 **cup all-purpose unbleached flour**

3 **teaspoons baking powder**

½ **teaspoon salt**

1 **cup quick-cooking oats**

1 **egg**

1 **cup milk**

½ **cup brown sugar, packed**

½ **cup raisins**

¼ **cup turbinado or raw sugar**

¼ **teaspoon cinnamon**

Preheat the oven to 400°F. Lightly grease 12 muffin cups with lard or line with paper baking cups; set aside.

In a large bowl, sift together the flour, baking powder, and salt. With a pastry blender, cut in the lard until the mixture resembles coarse crumbs. Stir in the oats.

In a separate large bowl, combine the egg, milk, and brown sugar; beat on low speed for 1 minute. Stir the egg mixture into the dry ingredients. Add the raisins and stir, being careful not to overmix.

Spoon the batter into the prepared muffin cups, filling two-thirds full. Combine the turbinado sugar and cinnamon in a small bowl; sprinkle evenly over each muffin. Bake for 20 to 25 minutes, until golden brown and a toothpick inserted in the center of a muffin comes out clean. Cool completely before serving.

HOT CROSS BUNS

An Easter tradition in historically Christian countries, hot cross buns are sweet, yeast-leavened rolls made with spices and dried fruit. The cross piped across the top with icing is a symbol of the crucifixion. For a different take on this classic, substitute dried cranberries or cherries (or a combination) for the raisins. Serve hot cross buns with butter and cheese. **Makes 16**

¾ cup warm milk

¼ cup plus 1 teaspoon granulated sugar

2¼ teaspoons active dry yeast

3¼ to 3½ cups all-purpose unbleached flour

1 teaspoon salt

1½ teaspoons cinnamon

½ teaspoon allspice

4 tablespoons lard, softened, plus more for greasing the pans

2 eggs, at room temperature

¾ cup raisins

2 teaspoons grated orange zest

GLAZE

1 egg

1 tablespoon milk

ICING

1 teaspoon milk

3 to 4 tablespoons confectioners' sugar

In a small bowl, stir together ¼ cup of warm milk and 1 teaspoon of sugar. Sprinkle the yeast over the milk and let sit for 5 to 10 minutes, until foamy.

In a large bowl, whisk together 3 cups of flour, the salt, cinnamon, allspice, and the remaining ¼ cup of sugar. Create a well in the flour and add the yeast mixture, lard, eggs, and the remaining ½ cup of warm milk. Using a large rubber spatula, mix the ingredients well. The mixture should be tacky and sticky. Stir in the raisins and orange zest.

Turn the dough onto a floured board and sprinkle a little flour over the top. Knead the dough, sprinkling more flour (1 tablespoon at a time), incorporating all the flour after each addition, and working in as much of the remaining ½ cup as possible. The dough should end up being slightly tacky but no longer completely sticking to your fingers. Place the dough ball in a greased bowl and cover with plastic wrap. Set in a warm place to rise for 2 hours, until doubled in size.

Turn the dough onto a floured board and punch down. Roll the dough into a log shape and cut it into 2 halves. Roll each half into a log, then cut each half into 8 equal pieces. Form the pieces into mounds. Grease two baking sheets with lard and place the buns on them 1½ inches apart (8 per sheet). Cover loosely with plastic wrap and let sit at room temperature to rise again, until the mounds have doubled in size, 30 to 45 minutes.

Using a very sharp knife or razor blade, score a cross pattern on the top of each bun (make deep cuts, or the pattern won't be noticeable after baking).

To prepare the glaze, whisk together the egg and milk. Using a pastry brush, brush the glaze over each bun.

Place the oven racks in the upper-middle and lower-middle positions. Preheat the oven to 400°F. Bake both sheets at once for 10 to 12 minutes, until the buns are lightly browned. Remove from the oven and let cool on the pan for a few minutes, then transfer the buns to a wire rack to cool completely.

To prepare the icing, whisk together the milk and the confectioners' sugar. Add more sugar until you have a consistency similar to a thick liquid or a thin paste. Place the icing in a plastic zip-top bag. Snip off a small piece (about ⅛ inch) from the corner of the bag and pipe the cross pattern on each bun.

OLD-FASHIONED VINEGAR ROLLS

You'd never guess from the name, but vinegar rolls are an old-time version of cinnamon rolls. The vinegar-and-sugar mixture forms a thick syrup in the bottom of the pan. By the time they're done cooking, the vinegar will have evaporated, leaving just a hint of tartness in the syrup. Serve hot with a pitcher of heavy cream, just like grandma did. **Makes 12**

⅓ cup lard, cold and coarsely chopped, plus more for greasing the pan

¾ cup apple cider vinegar

1½ cups water

1¼ cups sugar

4 teaspoons cinnamon

2 cups all-purpose unbleached flour

3 teaspoons baking powder

1 teaspoon salt

¾ cup milk

4 tablespoons unsalted butter

Preheat the oven to 375°F. Lightly grease a deep 13 by 9-inch baking dish with lard and set aside.

In a heavy saucepan, combine the vinegar, water, 1 cup of sugar, and 2 teaspoons of cinnamon. Cook over low heat, stirring continually, until the sugar dissolves; increase the heat to medium and cook for 20 minutes. Remove from the heat and allow to cool slightly.

In a large bowl, sift together the flour, baking powder, and salt. Cut in the lard until the mixture resembles coarse crumbs. Stir in the milk with a fork until a soft dough forms.

Turn the dough onto a floured board and roll out into a rectangle about ¼ inch thick. In a small bowl, combine the remaining ¼ cup of sugar and the remaining 2 teaspoons of cinnamon; evenly sprinkle the mixture over the surface of the dough. Dot with 2 tablespoons of the butter. Starting with the longer side, roll up the dough. Cut crosswise into slices about 1¼ inches thick. Place the rolls in the prepared baking dish and dot with the remaining 2 tablespoons of butter.

Evenly pour the hot vinegar mixture over the rolls. Bake for 30 to 40 minutes, until puffed and golden and the liquid has thickened to a syrup. Remove from the oven and loosen the rolls from the sides of the pan. Turn the pan of rolls upside down onto a serving platter so the syrup runs down and coats the rolls. Serve hot, fresh from the oven.

MA'S WONDERFUL BISCUITS I remember my Grandmother Viola Johnson's wonderful biscuits. She always made them with lard that she rendered herself. Her biscuits were the best ever.

Grandmother had ten children and many grandchildren, and she always had some of her wonderful biscuits in the warming cabinet of her woodstove, with homemade butter on the table to go with them.

Everyone related called her "Ma," and she made every one of us feel loved. I will never forget my grandmother. She died in 1970, but she is still my favorite cook, and not just because of her wonderful lard biscuits.

J. Steve Johnson,
Hiddenite, North Carolina

The attached picture of Ma and me was probably taken in the spring of 1947.

EVERLASTING ROLLS

These basic yeasted rolls are made with potatoes—beloved for the soft and fluffy texture they impart and the slightly sweet-and-sour flavor. They're "everlasting" because you can keep the dough in the refrigerator for up to one week. Bake them all at once for a crowd, or pinch off just what you need and serve them all week with supper. Makes 3 dozen

2¼ teaspoons active dry yeast

3 cups lukewarm water

1 cup mashed potatoes (without added butter or milk), lukewarm

1 cup lard, melted and cooled to lukewarm

1 cup sugar

1 tablespoon salt

1 teaspoon baking powder

6 to 8 cups all-purpose unbleached flour

Melted salted butter, for brushing

Butter and honey, for serving

Dissolve the yeast in the lukewarm water. In a large bowl, combine the potatoes, lard, sugar, salt, baking powder, and 3 cups of flour; add the dissolved yeast in water and stir well to combine. Cover with plastic wrap and let stand in a warm place for 30 minutes.

Turn the dough onto a floured board and knead in enough of the remaining flour to make a stiff dough. Knead for about 10 minutes until you have a smooth, elastic dough. Cover with plastic wrap and set in a warm place for about 2 hours. Then punch down and let rise again until doubled in size, about 1 hour.

At this point you can bake the rolls or refrigerate (see Note) the dough for use within 7 days.

To bake, roll into balls about 1½ inches in diameter. Grease a deep baking pan with lard and place the rolls, about 1 inch apart, in it. Cover with plastic wrap and set the pan in a warm place for about 15 minutes to let the rolls rise again. Brush the tops of the rolls with melted butter. Place the rolls in a cold oven and turn the temperature to 400°F. Set the timer for 25 minutes and bake until puffed and golden brown. Serve hot with butter and honey.

NOTE: If the dough has been refrigerated, remove the desired quantity from the refrigerator 90 minutes before baking and roll into balls; bake as instructed.

HOMEMADE FLOUR TORTILLAS

If you've never looked over the ingredients list on a package of store-bought tortillas, you should—it's an inch long. Forgo the plethora of additives and make your own—authentically made with lard—from pure ingredients. Serve warm with butter and honey for a snack, or with fixings for burritos or wraps for a meal. **Makes 12**

3 cups all-purpose unbleached flour

2 teaspoons baking powder

1 teaspoon salt

4 to 6 tablespoons lard, cold and coarsely chopped

1¼ cups warm water

In a large bowl, combine the flour, baking powder, and salt. Using a pastry blender, cut in the lard until the mixture resembles coarse crumbs.

Add the warm water a little at a time until the dough is soft and no longer sticky (do not use hot water).

Turn the dough onto a floured board and knead for a few minutes until it's soft and pliable. Divide the dough evenly into 12 golf ball–sized balls. Cover with a cloth and let the dough rest for 10 minutes or longer.

Dust each ball with flour and roll out with a rolling pin or palote as thinly as possible without tearing (¹⁄₁₆ inch or thinner).

Heat a griddle, comal, or cast-iron skillet over medium-high heat. (Do not use a very hot griddle or the tortillas will cook too quickly.)

One at a time, lay a tortilla on the hot griddle. Let it brown for a few seconds on one side, then turn it over. Each side should be nicely speckled.

After browning, place the tortilla on a towel or in a tortilla warmer and cover. Serve warm.

BLUEGRASS HUSH PUPPIES

These Southern-style hush puppies are the real deal. The buttermilk and minced onion deliver a flavor punch and help thwart their reputation for blandness. Mix up a simple dipping sauce of equal parts sour cream and mayonnaise with a few dashes of hot sauce for a crowd-pleasing appetizer—true Southern hospitality! **Makes 25**

2 cups finely ground cornmeal

1 teaspoon salt

1 teaspoon baking powder

¼ teaspoon baking soda

1 egg, slightly beaten

½ cup water

½ cup buttermilk

½ cup minced onion

Lard, for frying

Sift together the cornmeal, salt, baking powder, and baking soda. Add the egg, water, buttermilk, and onion; mix until blended.

In a cast-iron kettle, heat the lard to 2 inches deep and 375°F. Drop the batter by teaspoonfuls into the hot lard and fry for 3 to 5 minutes until golden brown, turning once halfway through the cooking time.

Remove the hush puppies from the fat with a slotted spoon and drain on paper towels. Allow to cool for 5 minutes before serving.

CAN'T FAIL WHOLE-WHEAT ROLLS

It can be difficult to achieve a tasty and fluffy whole-wheat roll, but these do that and with no more effort than recipes calling for all-purpose flour. Eggs help keep the rolls moist inside and the melted lard will deliver a crisp, flaky crust so delicious your guests will ask for seconds and thirds. Serve hot from the oven with honeyed or herbed butter. **Makes 2½ to 3 dozen**

4½ teaspoons active dry yeast

2 cups lukewarm water

½ cup sugar

3 teaspoons salt

3 cups whole-wheat flour

½ cup lard, melted and cooled slightly, plus more for greasing the pan

3 eggs

3½ cups (more or less) all-purpose unbleached flour

In a large bowl, dissolve the yeast in the lukewarm water and let sit for 5 minutes.

Add the sugar, salt, and 2 cups of the whole-wheat flour and beat with an electric mixer on medium-low speed until smooth. Add the lard and eggs, and beat until well combined.

Add the remaining 1 cup of whole-wheat flour and 3 cups of the all-purpose flour and stir to form a ball. Turn the dough onto a floured board and knead until it's soft, pliable, and easy to handle. Knead in as much of the remaining ½ cup of flour as possible.

Place the dough in a greased bowl, turning once to coat. Cover with plastic wrap and set in a warm place to rise until it's more than doubled in size, 2 hours or longer.

Preheat the oven to 350°F. Grease a baking sheet or two muffin tins with lard.

Pinch off the dough and shape into rolls about 1½ inches in diameter. Place on the prepared sheet or in the tins and cover with plastic wrap; set in a warm place to rise until light and airy, 20 to 30 minutes.

Uncover and bake for 20 to 25 minutes, until browned. Serve hot.

GRANNY'S GOOD COOKING

When my granny was eighty-seven years old, I was moving from Georgia to Arkansas and wanted to spend some time with her because I would soon be so far away. I was worried that due to her age and my financial concerns I might not have another chance to spend time with her.

She lived with one of her sons, his wife, and their two sons. I made arrangements to spend the weekend with her.

The first morning Granny asked me what I wanted for breakfast. I protested that she didn't have to cook for me. In a stern voice, Granny said, "What's the matter? Isn't my cooking good enough for you anymore?"

I immediately recognized my error. At the grand old age of twenty-five, I was not about to argue with Granny. Besides, she was a grand cook.

I immediately asked her for some of her biscuits. I told her that I had tried many times to duplicate her biscuits but just couldn't succeed. She consoled me with the news that it took her about six months to learn to make a passable biscuit after my aunt asked her to quit using lard in her cooking and to use solid shortening instead.

I am so glad to see this resurgence now in the use of lard.

As it turns out, I had several opportunities to visit Granny after I moved to Arkansas. She was just a few days shy of reaching ninety-nine when she left us. Her mind was sharp to the last, and I'll always treasure the special weekend I spent with her.

Over the years, I have bought lard to make my baked goods better for special holiday cooking, and I always thank Granny for the good cooking tip.

Linda Purcell, via e-mail

BUTTERSCOTCH ROLLS

Make these dressed-up cinnamon rolls for your next superspecial occasion, as that's how they're best described. The butterscotch, cinnamon, sugar, and butter conspire to create the ultimate comfort-food experience, all rolled up in a familiar package. **Makes 16**

1 cup milk

¼ cup lard, chilled, plus more for greasing the pan

½ cup sugar

1 teaspoon salt

2¾ cups all-purpose unbleached flour

2¼ teaspoons active dry yeast dissolved in ¼ cup warm water

4 tablespoons salted butter, softened

½ teaspoon cinnamon

1 (6-ounce) package butterscotch chips

¼ cup light corn syrup

2 tablespoons water

½ cup chopped walnuts

In a small saucepan, gently heat the milk to warm. Remove from the heat and add the lard, ¼ cup of sugar, and the salt and stir; let cool to lukewarm.

Transfer the milk mixture to a large bowl. Add 1 cup of flour and the dissolved yeast and stir to combine. Stir in the remaining 1¾ cups of flour to form a soft dough.

Turn out the dough onto a floured board and knead until it's soft and pliable, 5 to 10 minutes. Place the dough in a greased bowl and turn once to coat. Cover with plastic wrap and set in a warm place to rise until doubled in size. Once doubled, punch down.

Turn out the dough onto a floured board and roll out to a 16 by 8-inch rectangle. Spread 2 tablespoons of butter evenly over the surface. Combine the remaining ¼ cup of sugar and the cinnamon; sprinkle the mixture evenly over the dough. Starting with the long side, roll up the dough and cut into 1-inch slices. Grease a 9-inch baking pan with lard and set the rolls inside.

In a double boiler or in a microwave, combine the butterscotch chips, corn syrup, water, and the remaining 2 tablespoons of butter and heat until the chips are melted; stir well until smooth. Remove from the heat and let cool slightly, about 15 minutes. Fold in the walnuts.

Pour the butterscotch mixture evenly over the rolls; cover loosely with plastic wrap and set in a warm place to rise until doubled in size.

Preheat the oven to 350°F. Bake for 30 minutes, until puffed and golden brown. Remove from the heat and let cool for 2 to 3 minutes. Loosen the rolls from the sides of the pan and gently invert on a serving plate. Serve warm.

ICED CINNAMON ROLLS

These cinnamon rolls call for an old-fashioned but time-honored method of making a sponge, which allows the dough to ferment and build extra flavor before being combined with the rest of the ingredients. These are large, bakery-style rolls, and the buttermilk icing is irresistible!

A decidedly modern trick for slicing the dough roll: Use unflavored, unwaxed dental floss to cleanly cut the dough into rounds; it's light enough to allow you to slice through the soft dough without squeezing out the filling. Makes 1 dozen

2¼ teaspoons active dry yeast

1 teaspoon salt

2 cups lukewarm water

8½ to 9½ cups all-purpose unbleached flour

1 cup granulated sugar

1 cup lard, chilled, plus more for greasing the pans

1 large egg, plus 2 egg yolks

½ cup cold water

½ cup salted butter, softened

¾ cup brown sugar, packed

2 tablespoons cinnamon

ICING

3 tablespoons cream cheese, softened

3 tablespoons buttermilk

1½ cups confectioners' sugar

¼ teaspoon vanilla extract

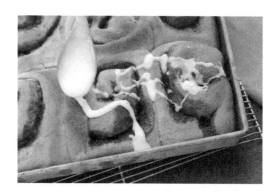

In a large bowl, combine the yeast, salt, lukewarm water, and 4 cups of flour. With a large rubber spatula, mix together thoroughly; the dough will be very sticky. Cover with plastic wrap and set in a warm place to rise for 2 hours. (This is the sponge.)

In a separate large bowl, cream together the granulated sugar and lard; add 2 cups of flour, one at a time, stirring well after each addition; the mixture will resemble pie dough.

In a small bowl, beat the egg and yolks with an electric mixer on medium-high speed until foamy, about 1 minute. Add the cold water to the eggs and stir to combine. Combine the 3 mixtures all at once in the sponge bowl and beat on low speed until smooth. Add enough additional flour (up to 2½ cups) to make the dough similar to the consistency of bread dough. Cover with plastic wrap and set in a warm place to rise, 1½ to 2 hours.

When doubled in size, turn the dough onto a floured board and knead until soft and pliable, about 10 minutes, adding up to 1 cup more of flour.

Roll out the dough to a 16 by 12-inch rectangle and a ⅓-inch thickness with a long side facing you. Using a rubber spatula, spread the butter evenly over the dough, leaving a ½-inch border at the far end.

Combine the brown sugar and cinnamon in a small bowl and mix with a fork. Sprinkle the mixture evenly over the dough.

Grease two 13 by 9-inch deep baking dishes with lard.

Starting with the long side closest to you, roll up the dough like a jelly roll, pinching with your fingertips as you roll. Moisten the top edge with water to seal the roll.

Using a sharp knife or dental floss (see recipe introduction), cut the roll into 12 equal slices; place 6 rolls, cut side down, close together in each dish. Cover loosely with a flour sack cloth or tea towel and set in a warm place to rise until doubled, 1½ to 2 hours.

Adjust the oven racks to the upper-middle and lower-middle positions. Preheat the oven to 350°F. Bake both dishes at the same time for 25 to 30 minutes, until golden brown; switch the positions of the dishes halfway through the baking time. Remove from the oven and let cool on a wire rack for 5 minutes.

To prepare the icing, place the cream cheese, buttermilk, and half the confectioners' sugar in a large bowl and beat with an electric mixer until smooth and free of lumps. Add the remaining sugar and the vanilla and beat. Using a tablespoon, drizzle the icing evenly over the rolls. Serve warm.

Chapter 2

VEGETABLES

ITALIAN SQUASH

Zucchini is a funny vegetable. We're always drawn to grow it in our gardens or buy it from the farmers' markets, but once it's home, we struggle with culinary creativity and it usually ends up being simply grilled or sautéed (not that there's anything wrong with that). Here's a dish you'll love for its ease and flavor, and for the fact that it turns an otherwise plain vegetable into a more substantial dish. Serve this alongside some grilled chicken for a chicken parmigiana–inspired meal. **Serves 6**

3 tablespoons lard

1 onion, peeled and diced

1 clove garlic, diced

2 pounds zucchini, sliced

¼ cup sliced celery

1 (8-ounce) can tomato sauce

½ teaspoon salt

½ teaspoon black pepper

½ cup grated Parmesan cheese

¼ cup bread crumbs

In a large skillet, heat the lard over medium-high heat. Add the onion and garlic; cook until tender, about 5 minutes. Add the zucchini and celery; cover and cook for 5 minutes, or until the squash is just tender.

Stir in the tomato sauce, salt, and pepper; mix gently. Sprinkle the mixture with the cheese and bread crumbs; cover and cook for 3 to 5 minutes, until heated through. Serve immediately.

OKRA with TOMATOES and OREGANO

Okra, a Southern delicacy, has definitely acquired a bad reputation. However, that reputation is mostly due to okra's being a victim of bad cooking. Its flavor is described as having hints of eggplant, green bean, and chestnut. The interior of an okra pod is mucilaginous, or sticky, and once cut open its juices will thicken the cooking liquid. This dish calls for the pods to be cooked whole, so the thickening effect will be slight. You may substitute frozen cut okra, but the sauce will be much thicker as a result. Serves 4

2 tablespoons lard

1 large yellow onion, peeled and sliced into wedges

½ teaspoon dried oregano leaves

1 (14.5-ounce) can stewed tomatoes

1 pound whole okra pods, washed and stemmed

Salt and black pepper

In a large skillet, heat the lard over medium-high heat. Add the onion wedges and sprinkle with the oregano; sauté until the onions are tender and translucent, about 5 minutes.

Stir in the tomatoes. Place the okra in the pan with the pods lined up side by side. Season with salt and pepper. Reduce the heat to low, cover, and simmer for 30 minutes, until the okra is tender. Serve immediately.

FRIED OKRA

The best okra, like most vegetables, is young and fresh straight from the garden. The plant becomes woody when mature, so pick the pods often and wash them just before cooking. Due to the chemical properties of iron, copper, and brass, okra will turn black when cooked in pans made from these metals. So put away the cast-iron skillet for this recipe and take out your stainless-steel model. **Serves 4**

1 pint okra, washed and cut into 1-inch pieces

⅓ cup evaporated milk

½ cup yellow cornmeal

Lard, for frying

Salt and black pepper

Line a baking sheet with wax paper and set aside.

In a large bowl, place the okra. Add the evaporated milk and mix until all the pieces are coated. In a medium bowl, place the cornmeal.

Working in batches, add a few pieces of the okra to the cornmeal and roll until well coated. Transfer the coated okra to the prepared baking sheet and refrigerate, uncovered, for 1 hour.

In a large skillet, heat the lard to 1 inch deep over medium-high heat until sizzling. Working in batches, fry the okra for 2 minutes, turning once, until browned. Drain on paper towels and season with salt and pepper. Serve immediately.

ROCKY MOUNTAIN GREEN BEANS

Green beans, fresh (if they could be had) or canned (more likely), smothered in a simple white sauce, was an often-requested dish of the cooks in the mining camps of the Rocky Mountains. Recreate that excitement in your kitchen with this dish. Double the recipe to feed your own legion of workers—they'll be asking for seconds. **Serves 6**

2 cups fresh or canned green beans

3 tablespoons lard

2 tablespoons minced onion

1 tablespoon minced green pepper

3 tablespoons flour

1 teaspoon salt

¼ teaspoon black pepper

½ teaspoon paprika

1 cup milk

1 pimiento, chopped

¼ cup grated Monterey Jack cheese

In a large saucepan, cook the green beans until tender. Reserve ½ cup of the cooking liquid, then drain the beans and set them aside.

In a large skillet, heat the lard over medium-high heat. Add the onion and green pepper and sauté for 2 minutes, until tender. Add the flour, salt, pepper, and paprika; stir well and cook for 3 minutes.

Gradually whisk in the milk and the reserved liquid from the beans. Cook over low heat, whisking constantly, until thick. Remove from the heat; add the pimiento and cheese, and stir until the cheese melts.

Place the cooked beans in a serving dish and pour the sauce over the top. Serve immediately.

LARDO SOUNDS MUCH MORE ROMANTIC

A couple of years ago I had the great fortune to take a trip to Italy for a couple of weeks as part of an international gathering of small farmers, food journalists, and restaurateurs. One of the young chefs came back from an outing wildly praising this unique treat he had found called lardo. Very delicate tasting, he said, very buttery, a cured pork product that is essentially the thick layer of fat taken from just below the pig's skin. Frankly, it sounded hideous, and I was certain he was either pulling our legs or had just tried it and decided to put one over on us by getting us to try something fundamentally gross. I was not the slightest bit interested.

However, a few days later, one of my friends and I found ourselves in a tiny out-of-the-way restaurant in Florence, and after studying the menu carefully for a few minutes, he ordered *lardo*.

The waitress looked skeptical and, I thought, a bit horrified. Just to make sure, she brought a little scrapbook with photos of all their dishes carefully displayed. Plainly they were accustomed to non-Italian speakers showing up hungry and clueless and had developed a point-and-order system.

She pointed to a large chunk of fat and said, "*Lardo.*"

"*Si, per favore,*" my friend replied. I ordered lovely, identifiable mushroom ravioli and sat back to watch this horror story unfold.

When it arrived, it was, indeed, lard. No doubt about it—a big chunk of lard—about the size of two sticks of butter and, I was certain, twice the number of calories.

(As it turns out, only a couple of grams more.) My friend took a slice with some crusty homemade bread and rolled his eyes with pleasure.

Then he sliced a little piece for me and insisted. I am nothing if not adventurous, so I held my breath, tore off a chunk of bread, and dutifully took a taste.

It was fabulous. If you've ever tasted pancetta or prosciutto, it was in that family of flavors: delicately hammy, well-salted, and with a gentle flavor of herbs and spices I couldn't identify. It was great with that bread, great with that wine, and, so help me, I had a second slice.

Now, my friend is about six feet tall and weighs about 30 pounds less than I do, so he could easily bear a little fattening up. I was committed to wearing the same size slacks when I left Italy as I had when I arrived, so I called it quits with my second little pat of *lardo*. My friend finished the entire chunk and most of a loaf of bread. And then we had salad.

I have since learned that lardo is indeed considered a delicacy in Italy. For many generations, it had been considered peasant food, but then gourmands from around Europe and across the pond locked their taste buds on it and suddenly lardo's reputation took a great leap forward. Luckily for our pocketbooks, this tiny bistro was too far off the beaten track to have gotten the news. Otherwise, we might have ended up washing dishes—all for the sake of a big chunk of lard.

K. C. Compton, GRIT *Executive Editor, Lawrence, Kansas*

OVEN-FRIED SWEET POTATO FRIES

If you've never made fries from sweet potatoes, you're in for a treat! Easy, and without the hassle of splattering fat, these fries are perfect for weeknight cooking. When sweet potatoes are roasted in this manner, the flavor is more concentrated than with other cooking methods, and the exterior becomes crisp and caramelized—a delicious combination. **Serves 4 to 6**

¼ cup lard, melted and cooled, plus more for greasing the pan

4 medium sweet potatoes, washed and dried, skin intact and blemishes removed

Kosher salt

Preheat the oven to 400°F. Grease a baking sheet with lard and set aside.

With a mandolin or a knife, cut the sweet potatoes lengthwise into ½-inch-thick strips. Place the sweet potatoes in a large bowl and toss with the lard. Arrange the potatoes in a single layer on the prepared baking sheet. Season with salt.

Bake for 30 to 40 minutes, until golden brown; using a thin metal spatula (so as not to tear the skins), turn the potatoes once after 20 minutes. Serve immediately.

POTATO PANCAKES

Potato pancakes, or latkes, are associated with the traditional foods of many countries—Ukraine, Belarus, Poland, Austria, Germany, Israel—but most commonly of Eastern Europe. Many different recipes—some with eggs and flour, some without—abound, but they're all similar in that the dish is always potato patties fried in fat (you could even sub leftover mashed potatoes or frozen hash browns in place of the grated potatoes). Serve salty with garnishes such as sour cream or cheese, or sweet with sugar and cinnamon or applesauce or jam. The Swedish version, called rarakor, is made with wheat flour and milk, and is traditionally served with fried bacon and lingonberry jam. Serves 8

2 eggs

2 cups grated raw potatoes

1 to 2 tablespoons grated onion

4 tablespoons all-purpose unbleached flour

1 teaspoon salt

¼ teaspoon black pepper

3 to 6 tablespoons lard

In a large bowl, beat the eggs; add the potatoes, onion, flour, salt, and pepper and mix well.

In a large skillet, heat 3 tablespoons of lard over medium-high heat until just sizzling. Using a tablespoon, drop the potato mixture into the hot fat and flatten with the back of the spoon. Work in batches and do not overcrowd the pan. Fry the pancakes until golden brown, about 2 minutes on each side. Drain on paper towels.

Repeat with the remaining batter, adding more lard as necessary. Keep the pancakes warm in the oven before serving.

OLD-FASHIONED GREEN BEANS

Yes, these are the green beans you'll get when you order them in small-town diners and roadside cafés. They're made the good old-fashioned way with bacon, brown sugar, and lard—a magical elixir of sorts. Serves 8

1 tablespoon lard

12 slices bacon, cut into ½-inch pieces

¼ cup dark brown sugar, packed

1½ cups water

2 pounds fresh green beans, trimmed and cut into 2-inch pieces

In a large skillet, melt the lard over medium heat. Add the bacon and fry, stirring frequently, 5 to 7 minutes, until browned.

Add the sugar and water; stir and mix well. Bring the mixture to a boil. Add the beans and reduce the heat to low. Cover and simmer for 50 to 60 minutes, until the beans are soft and all the liquid has been absorbed. Serve immediately.

SWEET ONION RINGS

Food historians really can't pinpoint the origin of the onion since it's so small and its tissues leave little, if anything, behind for archaeologists. Some say the earliest cultivation took place in the Mediterranean, others say it first grew in central Asia, while others say Iran. Celebrate its mysterious origins by whipping up an exotic dipping sauce: Whisk together 3 tablespoons of mayonnaise, 2 tablespoons of Dijon mustard, juice of half a lime, and 2 teaspoons of soy sauce. For some heat, mix in 2 teaspoons of prepared horseradish. **Serves 4**

1 cup all-purpose unbleached flour

1 teaspoon salt

1½ teaspoons baking powder

1 egg, separated

¾ cup milk

1 tablespoon peanut oil

Lard, for frying

3 to 4 large sweet onions, sliced into ½-inch rings

Kosher salt

In a medium bowl, whisk together the flour, salt, and baking powder. Set aside.

In a separate bowl, beat the egg yolk with an electric mixer; stir in the milk and oil. Stir in the flour mixture all at once.

In a small bowl, beat the egg white on high speed until soft peaks form; fold into the batter but do not overmix.

In a deep cast-iron skillet, heat the lard to 360°F and 1 inch deep. Working in batches, dip the onion rings in the batter using a fork and place in the hot fat without crowding. Fry for 1 to 2 minutes on each side, until golden brown. Drain and cool on paper towels. Season to taste with the salt.

CARROT FRIES

Carrots are a pantry staple for most everyday cooks. They're versatile and they'll store practically indefinitely in the refrigerator. Here's a new way to fix them that you've probably never considered: fried, just like potatoes. And rather than the obligatory bottle of ketchup, whisk together this dipping sauce to serve alongside: ⅓ cup of mayonnaise, 3 tablespoons of ketchup, 2 tablespoons of minced chives, a dash of hot sauce, and a pinch of salt.   Serves 6

2 eggs, well beaten

1 cup finely crushed cracker crumbs

Lard, for frying

1 pound carrots, peeled and cut into ¼-inch-thick sticks, 2 inches long

Kosher salt

In a small bowl, beat the eggs. Pour the cracker crumbs onto a small plate.

In a deep cast-iron skillet, heat the lard to 360°F and ½ inch deep.

Working in batches, using a fork, dip the long, tapering carrot sticks in the eggs, then roll in the cracker crumbs. Set the carrots in the hot fat without crowding; fry for 1 to 2 minutes on each side, until golden brown. Cover the pan tightly; lower the heat and cook gently for 10 minutes.

Drain and cool on paper towels. Season with salt and serve immediately.

FRIED CAULIFLOWER OMELET

This is a tasty and fun way to serve up cauliflower, broccoli, or asparagus. With the additions of eggs, cracker crumbs, and cheese, you've got a quick and complete meal for two or a side dish for four morning, noon, or night. Serve with ketchup or hot sauce on the side. Serves 4

1 small head cauliflower, washed and separated

Salt

2 eggs

¼ cup finely crushed cracker crumbs

½ cup grated cheese of your choice

Pinch of black pepper

3 tablespoons lard

In a large saucepan, boil or steam the cauliflower in salted water until just tender; drain and set aside to cool slightly.

In a large bowl, lightly beat the eggs; add the cracker crumbs, cheese, and pepper and mix well. Stir in the cauliflower.

In a medium skillet, heat the lard over medium-high heat until just sizzling. Pour in the cauliflower mixture and fry like an omelet, until golden brown and the eggs are set. Serve immediately.

RENDERING LARD My grandma always used lard in her cooking, and her food always tasted the best. Her fried chicken was especially good, and there is just nothing like potatoes fried in lard! She also used it to make pie crusts.

Nowadays, if we happen to process a hog, or know someone who does, we get the fat to render into lard. We don't do large amounts, and I'm not sure if there is a right or wrong way to do it, but here is what I do: I cut the fat into small chunks and put it into a pot. I turn it to a low temperature on the stovetop until it starts to melt. Then I turn the temperature up a bit and stir regularly until the fat cooks down and I am left with mostly liquid. I don't use a lard press. When I think the pieces have cooked down as far as they can, I simply strain the whole works through a fine colander.

The hardened pieces that are left go to the birds, and they pick them up quickly!

Lori Dunn, Mount Pleasant Mills, Pennsylvania

FRENCH-FRIED CUCUMBERS

Cucumbers are 90 percent water, so it's a good idea to dry them out a little before cooking. After peeling and slicing the cucumbers, place them in a colander with a teaspoon of salt and allow them to drain for 30 minutes; rinse and dry them thoroughly before preparation. Make an Asian-inspired dipping sauce (similar to the sauce used on cucumber salads at Japanese restaurants) by whisking together ¼ cup of soy sauce, 2 tablespoons of rice vinegar, 2 tablespoons of mirin (sweetened sake, available in the international food aisle of the supermarket), ¼ teaspoon of crushed red pepper flakes, 1 teaspoon of toasted sesame oil, and 1 scallion, white and green parts, minced. Serves 8

1 cup finely crushed cracker crumbs

Salt and black pepper

3 egg yolks, beaten

Lard, for frying

4 large cucumbers, peeled and sliced into ½-inch rounds

In a small bowl, place the cracker crumbs and season with salt and pepper; mix well. In a separate bowl, place the egg yolks and beat well.

In a medium skillet, heat the lard to 350°F and 1 inch deep. Working in batches, dip the cucumber slices in the egg yolks, then roll in the crumb mixture. Fry in the hot fat until golden brown, 1 to 2 minutes on each side. Drain on paper towels and serve immediately.

Grandma's Homemade Biscuits, page 2

Cranberry Quick Bread, page 12

Homemade Flour Tortillas, page 28

Iced Cinnamon Rolls, page 34

Oven-Fried Sweet Potato Fries, page 44

Old-Fashioned Green Beans, page 46

Sweet Onion Rings, page 47

Corn-Stuffed Peppers, page 57

FIRM EGGPLANT

Beneath an eggplant's purple skin lies pure white flesh with a spongy texture and a slightly bitter taste. It's important to eat eggplants soon after picking since they'll become even more bitter as time passes. Here's how to reduce the bitterness in eggplant: Prior to cooking, slice the eggplant and place in a bowl of water. Add a handful of salt, stir, and allow it to stand for 2 hours or overnight in the refrigerator. When ready to use, rinse the slices and pat dry. Serves 4

Lard, for frying

1 large eggplant, washed and cut into ¼-inch-thick slices, patted dry

Salt and black pepper

Herbs of your choice, such as oregano, thyme, mint, or cilantro

In a medium skillet, heat the lard to ½ inch deep over medium-high heat until sizzling. Working in batches, fry the eggplant for 1 to 2 minutes on each side, until browned.

Drain on paper towels and season with salt, pepper, and dried or fresh herbs of your choice. Serve immediately.

NOTHING BETTER THAN NATURE
It always amuses me to see food fads come full circle. Eggs, milk, butter, and many other things have come under the scrutiny of expert nutritionists. It seems that manufacturers just can't come up with a better product than Nature. Imagine that. Sensible eating seems to balance out over the long run. I've decided to stay away from anything that gets processed and put in a bag or a box as much as I can this year.

My dad claims to have used lard for butter during the Depression. I can remember cutting the hog lard up in chunks on hog-processing day when I was maybe five or six. I can't really remember what happened to it after I cut it up. Mom always made the best apple pies, and it was probably because of the lard in the crust. All this talk about pies is making me hungry.

I long for some of the simple ways of my youth. Then again, I can definitely do without the outhouse.

David J. Bentz, Omaha, Nebraska

FRIED POTATOES DELUXE

"Deluxe" here refers to the simple, but indulgent addition of heavy cream. What isn't made better with cream? Serve these crispy, creamy, old-time hash browns with ketchup or hot sauce, applesauce or jam. Serves 4 to 6

4 cups shredded raw potatoes

2 tablespoons heavy cream

¾ teaspoon salt

Dash of black pepper

Dash of paprika

2 tablespoons lard

In a large bowl, combine the potatoes and cream; add the salt, pepper, and paprika and mix well.

In a large skillet over medium-high heat, heat the lard until just sizzling. Pour in the potato mixture and spread it evenly over the pan; cover tightly. Reduce the heat to low and cook until browned on the bottom, about 5 minutes. Remove the lid, turn the potatoes, and cook, uncovered, until the other side is browned, about 10 minutes.

Transfer to a serving plate and serve immediately.

LARD WAS THE LEAST OF IT

I remember so many great tastes from my grandparents' Kansas farm. They were almost entirely self-sufficient when it came to the family's food. Grandma rendered her lard on the kitchen stoves (one was electric and one burned wood and corncobs), using a huge, black iron kettle that spanned two burners.

There was delicious pork and bacon, of course. All food scraps and extra milk from the cows went in the slop bucket on the front porch until someone took it across the lane to the pigs every day. I helped butcher the chickens sometimes, which wasn't much fun, but the Sunday dinners of chicken with homemade noodles were out of this world. I still make chicken and noodles today; my noodles are as good as Grandma's, but the flavor of my chicken is never as rich as I remember hers being.

Then there was her homemade cottage cheese, finished off with cream fresh from the hand-cranked separator. And there was slow-cooked oatmeal, again topped with cream that gave it a flavor most folks who haven't lived on a farm have never tasted. (Nobody worried about cholesterol and saturated fat back then—and everyone got more than enough exercise every day.)

There were two orchards with apples, pears, mulberries, plums, peaches, and even apricots. Grandpa kept honeybees and lots of hens for fresh eggs and meat. They grew a huge vegetable garden, of course, with Country Gentleman sweet corn and Rutgers tomatoes. One of my favorite chores was to run outside and go down into the earthy-smelling root cellar under the nearby milk house to get whatever Grandma needed for dinner from their stashes of potatoes, beets, carrots, apples, and a huge array of canned goods. (There were always black and yellow salamanders hiding under the crates.)

There were hollyhocks and Johnny-jump-ups outside the front door. In my garden today, I have a thorny shrub rose that once thrived in Grandma's flower garden. It literally explodes with yellow flowers every spring.

Life on the Kansas prairie was hard in some ways, I'm sure, but the flavors of the homegrown ultrafresh foods were extraordinary—and those flavors often involved the use of lard. Most of us today don't know what we're missing.

Cheryl Long, Mother Earth News Editor in Chief, Topeka, Kansas

HOMEMADE POTATO CHIPS

The best tool for the job of slicing potatoes potato chip–thin is a mandolin. Set the wheel to the thickness you need, and slice away with the comfort of knowing there's a substantial hunk of plastic between the blade and your knuckles. Use any kind of potato you like: russets, Yukon Golds, even fingerlings. After making your own chips, you'll pass up the supermarket version more often than you think. Serve these with a homemade ranch dip for your next get-together.
Serves 4

4 medium potatoes, peeled and sliced ¹⁄₁₆ inch thick

Lard, for frying

Salt

Place the sliced potatoes in a large bowl of cold water and soak for 30 minutes (this will remove excess starch and help them fry very crispy). Drain the potatoes and dry them thoroughly on a towel.

In a deep cast-iron skillet or Dutch oven, heat the lard to 350°F and 2 inches deep. Working in batches, drop in the potatoes in a single layer and fry until golden brown all over, about 3 minutes total per batch.

Drain on paper towels and season with salt. Cool completely before eating—they will crisp up as they cool. Store in an airtight container for up to 2 days.

FRIED GREEN TOMATOES

A Southern classic, fried green tomatoes make excellent use of late-season tomatoes that will never ripen before the first frost hits. When a killing cold snap is imminent, gather up all your green tomatoes and plan on having the family over for a fried tomato feast. Serve with cocktail sauce, ranch dressing, or as the "T" in a BLT sandwich. Serves 4

4 green tomatoes, sliced ¼ inch thick

Salt

½ cup all-purpose unbleached flour

3 tablespoons sugar

2 eggs

1 cup milk

Lard

Place the tomato slices in a large bowl of salted water. Soak for 4 hours. Drain, rinse, and pat dry.

Combine the flour, sugar, and eggs with enough milk (up to 1 cup) to make a thin batter.

In a large, deep skillet, heat the lard to 360°F and 2 inches deep. Working in batches and using a fork, dip the tomatoes in the batter and drop into the hot fat in a single layer. Fry for 2 minutes on each side, until crisp and golden brown.

Drain on paper towels and serve immediately.

STUFFED MUSHROOMS

There are as many recipes for stuffed mushrooms as there are for potato salad or coleslaw. Regardless, stuffed mushrooms are always a popular, crowd-pleasing party dish. These are slightly different than the usual bread crumb–coated varieties—they're braised in a spicy tomato sauce for extra flavor. Serves 8

2 tablespoons lard, plus more for greasing the pan

2 (6-ounce) cartons medium-sized white mushrooms, rinsed and dried

2 tablespoons Parmesan cheese

Salt, black pepper, garlic powder, and onion powder

1½ cups Italian-flavored bread crumbs

2 (8-ounce) cans tomato sauce

Preheat the oven to 350°F. Grease a 13 by 9-inch shallow baking dish with lard and set aside.

Remove the stems from the mushrooms and finely dice the stems.

In a large skillet, heat the lard over medium-high heat. Sauté the diced stems for 5 minutes until soft, stirring occasionally. Remove the pan from the heat; stir in the cheese and seasonings. Gradually add the bread crumbs and mix just until the mixture sticks together.

In another bowl, place the tomato sauce; season with the spices and mix well.

Pour half the sauce into the prepared baking dish, coating the bottom. Fill each mushroom cap with the bread crumb mixture and place in the dish. Dot the tops of the stuffed mushrooms with a little sauce. Add the remaining sauce to the bottom of the dish.

Cover the dish with aluminum foil and bake for 20 to 25 minutes. Remove the foil and bake an additional 30 minutes, until the mushrooms are tender and the stuffing is heated through. Serve immediately.

CORN-STUFFED PEPPERS

When you've got sweet corn and peppers coming in from the garden at the height of summer, turn to this classic combination for good in-season eating. Play around with the spices for variation, substituting whatever fresh herbs you've got growing outside.   Serves 4

4 tablespoons lard, plus more for greasing the pan

1 tablespoon chopped onion

1 tablespoon chopped red bell pepper

3 tablespoons all-purpose unbleached flour

1½ teaspoons salt

1 tablespoon sugar

1 teaspoon dry mustard

⅛ teaspoon cayenne

1 cup milk

1½ cups fresh corn

1 egg, slightly beaten

2 green bell peppers, halved, membranes and seeds removed

⅔ cup panko crumbs

¼ teaspoon paprika

In a large skillet over medium-high heat, heat 3 tablespoons of lard. Add the onion and bell pepper; sauté for 5 minutes, stirring constantly.

In a small bowl, whisk together the flour, salt, sugar, mustard, and cayenne; add to the onion and pepper, mixing well until moistened. Cook for 3 minutes, stirring constantly. Gradually pour in the milk, whisking constantly with each addition; bring to a boil. Lower the heat and stir in the corn and egg; cook for 5 minutes, stirring constantly. Remove from the heat and let cool for 10 minutes.

Preheat the oven to 400°F. Grease a 2-quart baking dish with lard and set aside.

When the vegetable mixture is cool, divide it evenly, spoon into the 4 pepper halves (about ½ cup per pepper half), and place the peppers in the prepared dish. Sprinkle the panko crumbs and paprika on top of the stuffed peppers and dot with the remaining 1 tablespoon of lard.

Bake for 20 minutes, until the peppers are heated through. Serve immediately.

VEGETABLE PIE

This pie is a special dish, with a flavor profile running the gamut from whole-wheat flour to miso to Parmesan cheese. Give yourself plenty of time for preparation, perhaps a lazy Sunday when the weather keeps you indoors and the family expects comfort food for supper. Miso can be found in the international foods aisle of most supermarkets. Serves 6

DOUGH

1½ cups all-purpose unbleached flour

¾ cup whole-wheat flour

¾ teaspoon salt

½ cup unsalted butter, chilled and coarsely chopped

4 tablespoons lard, cold and coarsely chopped

6 tablespoons (more or less) ice water

FILLING

1 pound winter squash (delicata, acorn, butternut, or buttercup), peeled, seeded, and diced

½ pound potatoes, diced

2 medium carrots, peeled and sliced

1 small head (6 to 8 ounces) broccoli, trimmed and separated into small florets

1 large stalk celery, diced

1 small red bell pepper, diced

1½ cups coarsely shredded cabbage

3 tablespoons unsalted butter

1 medium onion, diced

¼ pound mushrooms, cleaned and sliced

2 cloves garlic, minced

3 tablespoons all-purpose unbleached flour

2 cups milk

2 to 3 teaspoons miso or vegetable stock base (optional)

¼ cup boiling water (optional)

Scant teaspoon crumbled thyme or marjoram leaves

½ cup grated Parmesan cheese

Salt and black pepper

Place the flours and salt in the bowl of a food processor fitted with a metal blade and pulse to combine. Add the butter and lard; pulse until the mixture resembles coarse crumbs. (If mixing by hand, combine the flours and salt in a large bowl, then cut in the butter and lard using a pastry blender.) Add 4 tablespoons of ice water and pulse (or mix with a fork). Add the remaining 2 tablespoons of water while the machine is running and process just until the dough comes together in a ball.

Turn the dough onto a lightly floured surface and press together into a ball. Pinch off large walnut-sized pieces of dough. Using the heel of your hand, flatten each piece. When all the dough has been flattened, gather it together and repeat the process.

Divide the dough into two parts and flatten into disks about 1 inch thick. Wrap each half in plastic and refrigerate for at least 30 minutes; the dough can be prepared and refrigerated up to 2 days in advance.

To prepare the filling, in a large pot fitted with a steaming basket, pour 2 inches of water in the bottom. Place the squash, potatoes, and carrots in the basket, cover, and heat the water to boiling; steam 8 to 10 minutes. Add the broccoli, celery, and bell pepper; steam for 4 to 5 minutes more. Add the cabbage and remove from the heat; drain well.

In a large skillet over medium-high heat, melt the butter. Sauté the onion for 3 to 4 minutes, until translucent. Add the mushrooms and sauté an additional 2 minutes. Add the garlic and sauté 1 more minute. Add the flour and stir for 3 to 5 minutes. Add the milk all at once and whisk as it thickens.

Place the miso in the ¼ cup of boiling water, if using, and add to the sauce. Cook until the sauce is just simmering and thickening. Add the thyme and Parmesan; season with salt and pepper, and cook 3 to 5 minutes more. Remove from the heat and set aside.

Preheat the oven to 400°F. Remove the dough from the refrigerator and let stand for 10 minutes.

Place the disks of dough on a lightly floured surface or pastry cloth and, using a rolling pin, roll out each one to a ⅛-inch thickness. Fit one crust into the bottom of a 10-inch pie plate; set the other crust aside.

Spoon half of the vegetables into the crust-lined pie plate, season with salt and pepper, then spoon half the sauce over all. Repeat with the remaining vegetables and sauce. Cover the dish with the remaining crust; trim and fold under the edges. Crimp the edges with a fork or flute with your fingers. Prick the top crust a few times with a fork.

Bake for 10 minutes; reduce the heat to 375°F and bake an additional 30 minutes, until the sauce is bubbling and the crust is golden brown. Cool on a wire rack for 5 to 10 minutes before cutting and serving.

TURNING THE CRANK

As a child, I helped turn the crank on the grinder, grinding fat from a butchered hog for rendering into lard to use in cooking. Rendering was a very hot job.

In a large pan, the ground fat was cooked over a hot fire on the kitchen range fueled by wood. As the fat melted, it was strained and drained into crocks or jars. That was the lard, and as it cooled, it hardened. The fat was kept cooking until there was nothing to drain off. What was left in the pan was called "cracklings" and was used with lye to make soap. The kitchen got pretty hot and had a strange odor after rendering lard.

The best pie crusts were made with lard, and it was also used for frying and cooking. Food was delicious when lard was used. Eventually a time came when butchering wasn't done at home; the animals were taken to the slaughtering plant. Then the time came when we were all told lard wasn't healthy.

When I quit using lard in cooking, I couldn't determine why things didn't taste as good as they used to. Then I woke up to the fact that I had quit using lard. We got accustomed to the taste of vegetable shortening, but I still reminisce about that good food, especially pie crusts.

I don't miss rendering lard, however.

Lucille Wohler, Clay Center, Kansas

CAJUN RED BEANS and RICE

Louisiana-style red beans and rice don't get any more authentic than this recipe, right down to the ham bone. It's the perfect dish to simmer slowly on the stove during a winter snowstorm, destined to warm everyone's bones. Pass a bottle of Tabasco around the table. Serves 6

3 tablespoons lard

1 large yellow onion, chopped

1 small green pepper, chopped

2 cups dried kidney beans, soaked overnight

1 large ham bone or other pork bone

1 clove garlic, minced

1 bay leaf

Salt and black pepper

2 tablespoons chopped parsley

1½ cups uncooked rice, prepared according to package directions

In a large cast-iron Dutch oven over medium-high heat, melt the lard. Sauté the onion and green pepper for 5 minutes. Add the beans and their soaking water plus additional water to make up 2½ quarts (10 cups) of liquid.

Add the ham bone, garlic, and bay leaf. Heat the soup to boiling; reduce the heat to low and simmer gently for 3 to 4 hours, until the mixture is creamy and most of the liquid has evaporated.

Remove from the heat. Season with salt and pepper; stir in the parsley. Remove the bay leaf and the ham bone, and serve immediately over rice.

FRESH CORN POTPIE

This unusual dish is not like a traditional potpie with a flaky top crust; it's more like corn and dumplings. The "dumplings" will turn out very tender and pastrylike when you use the pastry flour. If you cannot get your hands on this specialty product, substitute ¾ cup of cake flour and ¾ cup of all-purpose unbleached flour for this recipe, and you'll get similar results. **Serves 6**

1½ cups pastry flour

¼ teaspoon salt

2 tablespoons lard, cold and coarsely chopped

1 egg, beaten

4 cups milk

2 cups fresh corn

3 tablespoons butter

Salt and black pepper

In a large bowl, sift together the flour and salt. Using a pastry blender, cut in the lard until the mixture resembles fine crumbs. Add the egg and mix until the dough sticks together.

Turn the dough onto a lightly floured board and roll out to a ¼-inch thickness. Using a knife, cut into 2-inch squares.

In a 6-quart Dutch oven, combine the milk, corn, butter, and salt and pepper to taste; heat to boiling. Drop in all of the dough squares and boil gently for 25 to 30 minutes, stirring frequently with a fork to keep the dough from sticking together. When done, the pastries should be puffed and doubled in size. Serve immediately.

SPINACH PATTIES

An antioxidant powerhouse, spinach is as nutritious as it is versatile. If you've always thought to serve it sautéed or wilted in a salad, try it fried, as in these patties; the lard helps the body assimilate the nutrients of the leafy greens. Spinach has a very high water content, so after parboiling (boiling for a minute, more or less), drain it and place it on paper towels; squeeze until all the water comes out; repeat on fresh paper towels. Now measure it and proceed with the preparation. Top the patties with a creamy dipping sauce made from equal parts mayonnaise and sour cream, minced shallots, and fresh or dried tarragon. **Makes 12 patties**

2 cups chopped parboiled spinach

1½ cups finely crushed cracker crumbs

2 eggs

1 tablespoon minced onion

1 tablespoon minced celery

2 tablespoons minced parsley

Lard, for frying

In a large bowl, combine the spinach, 1 cup of the cracker crumbs, 1 egg, the onion, celery, and parsley; mix well. Using a ¼-cup measuring scoop, make 12 small patties. In a small bowl, beat the remaining 1 egg and place the remaining ½ cup of cracker crumbs on a small plate.

In a large skillet over medium-high heat, heat the lard to ½ inch deep and sizzling. Working in batches, dip the patties in the egg, then dredge in the cracker crumbs. Place in the hot fat without crowding, and fry for 2 minutes on each side, until golden brown.

Drain on paper towels and serve immediately.

ZUCCHINI PATTIES

Zucchini has a high water content, so to avoid soggy patties, remove as much excess moisture as possible before frying. After grating the zucchini, place it in a colander, add a teaspoon of salt, and let it drain for 15 to 30 minutes; rinse with cool water and dry thoroughly before combining the ingredients. Serve these crispy patties with a garden salad tossed in Italian dressing for a light summertime meal. Serves 8

3 cups grated zucchini

1 medium onion, grated

1 large clove garlic, minced

1 teaspoon salt

¼ teaspoon black pepper

1 egg, slightly beaten

3 heaping tablespoons all-purpose unbleached flour

Pinch of thyme

Lard, for frying

1 cup grated cheddar cheese

In a large bowl, combine the zucchini, onion, garlic, salt, pepper, egg, flour, and thyme; mix well.

In a large skillet over medium-high heat, heat the lard to ½ inch deep and sizzling. Using a large spoon, drop in the zucchini mixture, flattening the patties slightly with a spatula. Fry for 2 to 3 minutes on each side, until browned. Remove the skillet from the heat.

Sprinkle the cheese over the top of the patties; cover the skillet and let stand until the cheese is melted. Serve immediately.

Chapter 3

MAIN DISHES

GREAT TEXAS HASH

Quick and very easy, this one-skillet wonder is the perfect recipe to turn to when you're tired after a long day and you've got lots of hungry mouths to feed. Use leftovers to make a beef potpie the next day. Serve with corn bread and a green salad. **Serves 4 to 6**

2 cups minced onion

3 tablespoons lard

1 pound ground beef

1 cup diced green pepper

4 cups diced canned tomatoes

¾ cup raw white rice, washed

1 teaspoon chili powder

1 teaspoon salt

¼ teaspoon black pepper

In a large skillet, sauté the onion in the lard. Add the ground beef and cook, stirring constantly and breaking up the meat, until browned.

Stir in the green pepper, tomatoes, rice, and spices. Cover and cook, stirring occasionally, until the rice is tender and the sauce has thickened, 30 to 45 minutes. Serve immediately.

CORN PONE PIE

Corn pone pie is a traditional southwestern dish—chili with corn bread on top—done here with a midwestern twist. The cornmeal crust complements the spicy ingredients and completes the meal. For an extra-special treat, grind your own cornmeal from dried Indian corn, or use coarsely ground cornmeal for a little crunch. Serve this pie with sour cream, green onions, and cilantro for garnish.   Serves 6

1 tablespoon lard, plus more for greasing the dish

⅓ cup chopped onion

1 pound ground beef

2 teaspoons chili powder

¾ teaspoon salt

1 teaspoon Worcestershire sauce

1 cup canned diced tomatoes

1 cup red beans, drained

CRUST

½ cup cornmeal

½ cup flour

⅛ cup sugar

¼ teaspoon salt

2 teaspoons baking powder

1 egg

½ cup milk

⅛ cup lard, cold and coarsely chopped

Preheat the oven to 400°F. Grease a 1½-quart casserole dish and set aside.

In a large skillet, sauté the onion and beef in the lard, stirring often, until the meat is cooked through. Add the chili powder, salt, Worcestershire sauce, tomatoes, and beans. Simmer gently, stirring occasionally, for about 15 minutes. Pour into the prepared casserole dish and set aside.

To prepare the crust, sift together the cornmeal, flour, sugar, salt, and baking powder. Add the egg, milk, and lard; beat with an electric mixer on low speed until the batter is smooth. Pour over the chili mixture.

Bake for 25 to 30 minutes, until the crust is golden brown. Serve immediately.

HUNGARIAN BARLEY STEW

This hearty and filling stew is distinctly Hungarian with its use of lard, paprika, onion, garlic, and slow-cooked meat, all prepared in a single pot. You'll appreciate this recipe after a cold, harried day as it's ready in less than an hour. Top each serving with sour cream and a hunk of crusty bread on the side, and you'll please even the pickiest eaters. Serves 8

2 tablespoons lard

1½ pounds beef chuck, cut into ½-inch cubes

1½ cups chopped onion

1 to 2 cloves garlic, minced

1 (28-ounce) can crushed tomatoes with juices

3 cups water

⅔ cup barley

2 cubes beef bouillon

1 tablespoon sugar

1 tablespoon paprika

½ teaspoon salt

¼ teaspoon caraway seeds

In a large (4-quart) saucepan, heat the lard over medium-high heat. Add the beef and cook until browned. Add the onion and garlic and cook for 5 minutes. Pour off the excess fat.

Stir in the tomatoes, water, barley, bouillon cubes, sugar, paprika, salt, and caraway seeds; heat to boiling. Reduce the heat to low; cover and simmer for 45 to 50 minutes, stirring occasionally, until the beef and barley are tender. Serve immediately.

REMEMBERING LIVER SAUSAGE

When my age was only a single digit, I remember my dad helping butcher a hog, and I also remember the ugly outcome. Butchering always happened when it was really cold. We were told to stay in the house and away from what the men were doing.

Not me. I had to see it all by peeking from an upstairs window. What a gory mess!

My mom cooked the pig head in a big pot, took all the usable meat pieces out, and ground it all for liver sausage and other meats to cook and can. That was OK, because I like liver sausage and remember the blood sausage as being good, too.

Mom's recipe for liver sausage was: using the meat from the head plus the heart and tongue, cook until done (I don't remember how long), and grind. Add salt, black pepper, allspice (I don't remember the amounts; probably just to taste), and fried onion. Mix until mushy, pack in jars, and cook for 3 hours. Using a special funnel, she also put some of the mixture in casings. Then the sausages were taken to the local butcher shop to be smoked or were smoked at home when we still had a smokehouse.

Headcheese was made almost the same way, only salt, black pepper, and raw onion were mixed together with the same consistency. I recall the taste was wonderful!

The lard was cut to fit into the big black frying pan and set on the old cookstove, probably heated with corncobs, to melt down—the process known as rendering lard. I don't remember when it was strained, but the leftover pieces in the bottom of the pan, called cracklings, were later reheated, and we enjoyed eating this treat hot with lots of salt for our supper meal.

The strained lard was put into small crocks, sliced onions added, the crocks set on the back of the stove and slowly cooked (no boiling because that made it too hot) until the onions were browned. The onions were sometimes removed and the lard chilled— outdoors, since we had no refrigerator—or put in the cellar. The lard was then spread like butter on homemade rye bread, salted, and enjoyed as part of our supper. We called this *schmaltz* (my spelling may not be right, but it sounds right).

EDITOR'S NOTE: Schweineschmalz *is the German word for* lard, *literally,* pig fat. Schmaltz *is rendered chicken fat, a staple of traditional Jewish cookery.*

Agnes Porter, Anaheim, California

BEEF WELLINGTON

While the origin of this dish is unclear—theories range from being named for England's Duke of Wellington to being invented for a civic reception in Wellington, New Zealand—"Wellington" is often used generically to describe any meat baked in puff pastry. Nevertheless, this dish honors one of the finest cuts of beef—the tenderloin. Make it for Christmas dinner or another special occasion during which guests will cherish the memory of this gustatory delight. **Serves 8**

2¼ pounds beef tenderloin roast

⅔ cup lard, cold and coarsely chopped, plus more for greasing the pan

2¼ cups all-purpose unbleached flour

½ teaspoon salt

2⅓ to 2½ cups cold water

1 (4.75-ounce) can liver pâté

1 egg, beaten

GRAVY

2 teaspoons instant beef bouillon granules

⅓ cup burgundy wine

½ teaspoon crushed dried basil

Salt and black pepper

Preheat the oven to 425°F. Rinse the beef in cold water and pat dry. Trim any excess fat or connective tissue. Place the tenderloin on a rack in a shallow roasting pan. Insert a meat thermometer into the center of the meat.

Roast the tenderloin for 45 minutes, or until the thermometer registers 130°F. Remove the roast from the pan; cover with aluminum foil and refrigerate while preparing the pastry. Reserve the drippings.

Grease a baking sheet with lard and set aside.

In a large bowl, combine 2 cups of the flour with the salt. Using a pastry blender, cut in the lard until the mixture resembles coarse crumbs. Add ⅓ to ½ cup cold water, 1 tablespoon at a time, tossing with a fork until moist. Gather the dough into a ball and transfer to a lightly floured surface. Roll the dough out to a 12 by 14-inch rectangle.

Evenly spread the pâté over the dough to within ½ inch of the edges. Center the tenderloin on the pastry and wrap the dough around the meat. Trim any excess pastry and pinch to seal. Brush the pastry with the beaten egg.

Place the meat roll, seam side down, on the prepared baking sheet. Roll out the remaining pastry scraps and cut in decorative shapes. Place the decorative pastry on the meat roll, pinch into place, and brush with the egg.

Bake for 35 minutes, until the pastry is golden brown and flaky. While baking, cover with foil to prevent overbrowning, if necessary.

While the roast is cooking, prepare the gravy. Transfer the reserved drippings to a small saucepan. Add 1½ cups of cold water and the bouillon granules. Over medium-low heat, cook and stir until the mixture is blended and the bouillon has dissolved. In a bowl, whisk together the remaining ½ cup of cold water with the remaining ¼ cup of flour; stir into the hot bouillon mixture. Add the wine and basil. Cook, whisking constantly, until thick, 1 to 2 minutes. Season to taste with salt and black pepper.

When the roast is done cooking, remove from the oven and let rest for 15 minutes. Slice the pastry-wrapped tenderloin into 8 slices; serve with a bowl of gravy and allow the diners to help themselves.

FIESTA BEEF POTPIE

This little creature of a pie is as delicious as it is beautiful. Flavors include everything from wheat germ and cheddar cheese in the crust to cubed beef chuck, crunchy corn, and fiery southwestern spices, all wrapped up in a pretty potpie package. Your guests will have no idea what awaits them inside. For garnish, serve with shredded cheddar cheese, sour cream, chopped green onions, and a bowl of salsa. Olé! Serves 8

CRUST

1⅔ cups all-purpose unbleached flour

⅓ cup yellow cornmeal

2 tablespoons toasted wheat germ

1 teaspoon salt

⅓ cup finely shredded cheddar cheese

¾ cup lard

5 to 7 tablespoons cold water

FILLING

1 tablespoon lard

1 pound lean boneless beef chuck, cut into ¼- to ½-inch cubes

½ cup chopped green pepper

½ cup chopped onion

1 (14.5-ounce) can diced tomatoes with juices

1 (8.5-ounce) can whole kernel corn, drained

1 (4-ounce) can chopped green chiles with juices

½ cup water

⅓ cup tomato paste

2 teaspoons sugar

1 teaspoon chili powder

½ teaspoon ground cumin

¼ teaspoon salt

⅛ teaspoon dried crushed red pepper

⅓ cup sliced black olives

GLAZE

1 egg, beaten

¼ teaspoon salt

To prepare the crust, combine the flour, cornmeal, wheat germ, and salt in a large bowl. Stir in the cheese. Using a pastry blender or two knives, cut in the lard until just blended, forming pea-sized chunks. Sprinkle with cold water, 1 tablespoon at a time, and toss lightly with a fork until the dough comes together in a ball. Divide the dough in half and place each half, cut side down, on a floured board. Flatten each half to form 5- to 6-inch rounds. Wrap one round in plastic and place in the refrigerator. Using a rolling pin, roll out the other round and fit into the bottom of a 9-inch pie plate. Refrigerate while you prepare the filling.

To prepare the filling, heat the lard in a large skillet over medium-high heat. Brown the beef, then transfer to a bowl using a slotted spoon. In the same skillet, add the green pepper and onion; sauté until just tender. Add the cooked beef, tomatoes, corn, green chiles, water, tomato paste, sugar, chili powder, cumin, salt, and crushed red pepper; stir well. Cover and bring to a boil. Reduce the heat to low and simmer for 30 minutes,

stirring occasionally. Remove from the heat and stir in the olives. Set aside to cool and thicken slightly.

Preheat the oven to 425°F.

Roll out the remaining dough to a 10-inch round to form the top crust. Spoon the cooled filling into the prepared unbaked pie crust. Moisten the overhanging pastry edge with water. Place the top crust over the pie; press and flute the edges to seal. Using a sharp knife, cut 4 steam vents, evenly spaced, on the top crust.

To prepare the glaze, whisk together the egg and salt. Brush lightly over the crust. Bake for 30 to 40 minutes, until the juices are bubbling and the crust is golden brown. Serve immediately.

BIEROCKS

Bierocks (BEE-rocks) are pastry pockets typically filled with beef, onions, and cabbage. They originated in Eastern Europe and were brought to America in the nineteenth century by German-Russian Mennonite immigrants. The Midwest, particularly Kansas and Nebraska, is now the bastion of bierocks, with even a regional fast-food chain (Runza) serving their version as their centerpiece.

Bierocks make great Oktoberfest fare. When they emerge from the oven, cut a slit in the top of each one and drop in a pat of butter. Serve with coarse mustard, German sausages, sauerkraut, and dark beer, of course, for an authentic German experience. Makes 1 dozen

DOUGH

2¼ teaspoons active dry yeast

1¼ cups warm water

¼ cup lard, softened, plus more
for greasing the pans

¼ cup sugar

1½ teaspoons salt

2 eggs

4 cups all-purpose unbleached flour

FILLING

1 teaspoon lard

1 pound ground beef

1 cup minced onion

4 cups chopped cabbage

1 teaspoon salt

¼ teaspoon black pepper

In a small bowl, soak the yeast in ¼ cup of warm water. In a large bowl, cream the lard with the sugar, salt, and eggs. Add the yeast to the remaining 1 cup of warm water and 2 cups of flour; mix well. Add the remaining flour gradually and stir until the dough comes together.

Turn the dough onto a floured surface and knead for 5 to 10 minutes until soft and smooth. Place the dough in a clean bowl and cover with plastic wrap; set in a warm place to rise until doubled, 1½ to 2 hours.

To prepare the filling, heat the lard in a large skillet over medium-high heat; add the beef and cook until browned, stirring constantly, about 5 minutes. Add the onion, cabbage, salt, and pepper; cook for 5 minutes, stirring constantly to keep the steam from building up moisture. Using a slotted spoon, transfer the mixture to a bowl and set aside.

Grease two baking sheets with lard and set aside.

When the dough has risen, turn it out onto a floured surface. Using a food scale, pinch off 3-ounce balls and roll out flat to about a ¼-inch thickness. Place ½ cup of the meat mixture in the center of each; pull the corners of dough over the filling and pinch tightly to seal. Place the *bierocks*, seam side down, 1 inch apart on the prepared baking sheets.

Preheat the oven to 375°F. Cover the *bierocks* loosely with plastic wrap or a towel to rise while the oven is heating.

Bake for 20 to 25 minutes, until golden brown. Serve warm or at room temperature. Freeze any leftovers.

BAKED STEAK

This easy and ingenious recipe originates with the frugal cook, and even calls for the versatile and ubiquitous can of cream of mushroom soup to prove it. Lean and moderately tough (read: "cheap") cuts of meat, such as round steak, dry out when cooked with dry-heat methods such as roasting or grilling. "Baked steak" is braised—a slow, moist-heat method that tenderizes the meat and maintains moisture. Serve with mashed potatoes and a side salad for a satisfying supper.   Serves 4

1 teaspoon salt

¼ teaspoon black pepper

¼ cup all-purpose unbleached flour

1 pound round steak, cut into 4-ounce serving pieces

2 tablespoons lard

¼ cup chopped onion

1 (10.75-ounce) can cream of mushroom soup

½ cup water

Preheat the oven to 325°F.

In a medium bowl, mix together the salt, pepper, and flour. Dredge the steak pieces in the flour mixture and set aside.

Melt the lard in a large skillet over medium-high heat; add the steak pieces and onion. Cook until the meat is browned and the onion is translucent, 5 to 10 minutes. Place in a 2-quart casserole dish.

Combine the soup and water in the same skillet used for the steak; stir until all the brown bits from the cooked meat are mixed with the liquid. Pour the "gravy" over the meat in the dish and cover tightly with aluminum foil.

Bake for 1½ hours, until the meat is tender.

LIVER PATTIES

Back in the day, organ meats, such as liver, were common fare and were regularly served once a week. Extremely rich in fat-soluble vitamins A and D, as well as essential fatty acids, liver is an important food for building strength and vitality. This old-fashioned recipe will ease you into the idea of eating this healthful source of protein and nutrients. Use a food processor with a metal blade or a stand mixer fitted with a meat-grinding attachment to grind the liver. Serves 4 to 6

1 pound beef liver, membrane removed, coarsely ground

¾ cup chopped onion

⅓ cup bread crumbs

1 teaspoon salt

⅛ teaspoon black pepper

2 tablespoons milk

2 eggs, lightly beaten

3 tablespoons lard

In a large bowl, combine the liver, onion, bread crumbs, salt, pepper, milk, and eggs; mix well.

In a large skillet, heat the lard over medium-high heat. Using a tablespoon, drop spoonfuls of the liver mixture into the hot fat and flatten slightly with a spatula. Fry until golden brown on both sides. Drain on paper towels and serve immediately.

MOCK CHICKEN-FRIED STEAKS

More like chicken-fried hamburgers, these are an easy and fun way to use up lots of ground beef, as this recipe can easily be multiplied to serve more people. And no running to the store—you've probably got all the ingredients in your pantry right now. Serve with homemade ranch dressing in lieu of the usual gravy. Serves 4

1 pound ground beef

2 teaspoons onion salt

2 teaspoons parsley flakes

1 egg

1 teaspoon salt

1 tablespoon chili powder

2 cups crushed Ritz crackers

Lard

In a large bowl, mix the ground beef with the onion salt, parsley flakes, egg, salt, chili powder, and 1 cup of the crushed crackers. Roll the seasoned meat into 4 equal-sized balls.

Sprinkle the remaining 1 cup of crushed crackers on a cutting board. Using your hand or a rolling pin, flatten the meatballs into steaks about ½ inch thick, making sure both sides are well coated with the crackers. Place the steaks on wax paper and chill for 30 minutes or longer.

In a large skillet, heat the lard to 1 inch deep over medium-high heat. Add the steaks and cook 6 to 7 minutes on each side, until both sides are nicely browned and the meat is cooked through.

MUSHROOM MEATBALLS

When Aunt Marge calls at 5:00 p.m. and asks, "What can you bring over for supper tonight?" this dish is an easy answer. Quick, easy, and without fuss, these meatballs can be browned in a skillet, cooked through, then tossed in a Crock-Pot for that impromptu car ride and dinner with the family. Makes 2 dozen

1 pound ground beef

⅔ cup fine bread crumbs

2 tablespoons dried minced onion

2 tablespoons dried chopped parsley

1½ teaspoons salt

1 egg, lightly beaten

2 (10.75-ounce) cans condensed cream of mushroom soup

¼ cup water

2 tablespoons lard

In a large bowl, combine the beef, bread crumbs, onion, parsley, salt, and egg; mix well and set aside. In a separate bowl, combine the soup and water; whisk until blended.

Add ¼ cup of the soup mixture to the beef mixture and mix well. Roll the meat into 1-inch balls; set aside.

In a large skillet, heat the lard over medium-high heat. In batches, cook the meatballs until browned. Lower the heat, pour the remaining soup mixture over the meatballs, and cover. Simmer for 30 minutes, until the meatballs are cooked through.

POTATO PAPRIKASH

This popular Hungarian heartland delight will surely spice up your next potluck. It's an easy one-pot dish that travels well in a Crock-Pot and satisfies all those hungry men in attendance.
Serves 8

1 teaspoon lard

1 cup chopped onion

3 cloves garlic, minced

1½ pounds new potatoes, cut into ¾-inch cubes

1 (14.5-ounce) can low-sodium chicken broth

1 (14.4-ounce) can sauerkraut, drained

1 (8-ounce) can tomato sauce

1 cup chopped green pepper

1 tablespoon paprika

½ teaspoon salt

1 pound fully cooked smoked turkey sausage, sliced into ½-inch rounds

In a large skillet, heat the lard over medium-high heat. Add the onion and garlic and sauté for 5 minutes. Add the potatoes and broth; cover and simmer for 15 minutes.

Stir in the sauerkraut, tomato sauce, green pepper, paprika, and salt; mix well. Add the sausage; cover and simmer for 10 minutes until fully cooked through. Serve immediately or transfer to a Crock-Pot and set on low heat (or warm) until serving.

MAKE-AHEAD CHILI

This vintage chili recipe originally called for the "liquid from 1 cooked soup bone," added for flavor. If you are industrious enough to procure that old-time ingredient, substitute it for the beef base below. The flavor of this chili is enhanced by letting it stand for a few hours or overnight, so make it on any Saturday evening in the fall, refrigerate, and reheat it on Sunday, just before kickoff. Serve with sour cream, grated cheese, and minced onions for garnish. Serves 8 to 10

5 tablespoons lard

2 large onions, chopped

3 cloves garlic, chopped

3 pounds ground beef

1 pound ground pork

3 tablespoons chili powder

3 teaspoons salt

1 teaspoon black pepper

2 quarts tomatoes, run through a sieve, or 1 quart tomato juice

1 (6-ounce) can tomato paste

1 teaspoon beef base or granules, dissolved in 2 cups hot water

6 cups cooked pinto beans

In a large skillet, heat the lard over medium-high heat. Add the onions, garlic, beef, and pork; sauté until the meat is browned and the onions are translucent, about 15 minutes. Drain.

Transfer the mixture to a large stockpot. Add the chili powder, salt, pepper, tomatoes, and tomato paste; then stir in the dissolved beef base; heat to boiling. Cover, reduce the heat to low, and simmer for 1 hour.

Add the beans and simmer for 1 hour longer, stirring frequently. Add more water as necessary.

HAMBURGER in CHEESE POPOVERS

Popovers are irresistible with their moist, airy centers and crisp, golden brown crusts. Traditionally served warm with butter and jam or—such as Yorkshire puddings—alongside roasted meats, here they help create an elevated version of Hamburger Helper. Your laughter will dissolve into a pleasant smile as the creamy hamburger and crispy pastry fill your mouth with savory goodness—the epitome of comfort food. Serves 6

5 tablespoons lard, plus 3 teaspoons for greasing the pan

1 pound ground beef

½ cup sliced onion

3 tablespoons plus 1 cup all-purpose unbleached flour

3 cups milk

¼ teaspoon salt

¼ cup grated cheddar cheese

1 tablespoon butter, melted

2 eggs, beaten

Place ½ teaspoon of lard into each cup of a 6-cup popover pan. Place the pan in a cold oven and preheat it to 450°F.

In a large skillet, melt 2 tablespoons of the lard over medium heat. Add the beef and onion slices; sauté for 10 minutes, until the meat is lightly browned and the onions are translucent. Drain.

In a saucepan, heat the remaining 3 tablespoons of lard over medium heat. Add 3 tablespoons of flour and stir vigorously; cook for 3 minutes. Gradually whisk in 2 cups of milk, whisking constantly, until the sauce is smooth and thickened. Add the sauce to the meat mixture and set aside, keeping it warm.

In a small bowl, sift together the remaining 1 cup of flour and the salt. In a separate bowl, combine the remaining 1 cup of milk, the cheese, and melted butter; add the eggs and the flour mixture and beat with an electric mixer on low speed for exactly 2 minutes, until smooth.

Once the oven has reached temperature, remove the hot pan and fill each cup two-thirds full with batter. Bake for 20 minutes; reduce the temperature to 325°F, and bake an additional 10 to 15 minutes, until the popovers are puffed and golden brown. Remove the pan from the oven and invert onto a wire rack.

Place one popover on each serving plate and split it open; fill with the creamed hamburger mixture. Serve immediately.

GOOD VS. BAD FAT

I discovered lard when I lived in Germany. I've never had fried potatoes that tasted as good as their Bratkartoffeln, potatoes and onions fried in lard. Absolutely scrumptious! And the flavor of Wiener schnitzel (breaded veal cutlets) fried in lard. I haven't yet found any so-called German restaurant in the United States that comes close to matching the flavor of real German cooking, so I've given up and I cook it myself.

These days, most of the lard I find has been hydrogenated, which is very unhealthy, so I have been rendering my own. We buy fat from the butcher at the local Mexican market and use our slow cooker to render the lard. The cracklings left over are good snack food and taste great on salads.

My better half was diagnosed with type 2 diabetes last year, and we've done a lot of research on diet since then. We've discovered that almost everything we've heard about diet over the last forty years or so is wrong. Natural animal fats—butter, lard, tallow, and the like—are good for you. Processed vegetable oils—trans fats—are very bad for you. Dietary cholesterol has absolutely no affect on your body's cholesterol levels—your body manufactures its own cholesterol, it doesn't use the cholesterol you eat. And so on and so forth.

Meanwhile, the Bratkartoffeln taste great.

Kim Ann Innes, Trenton, Texas

HENRIETTA'S SPICY FRIED CHICKEN

When Memphis-born Henrietta relocated to Lincoln County, Kansas, to be with her husband after the war, she found herself smack-dab in the middle of bland … bland food, that is. So she took her mother-in-law's fried chicken recipe and gave it some zing to create this spicier version. Serve with your favorite potato salad and coleslaw for the perfect summertime picnic. Serves 4 to 6

1 to 2 teaspoons black pepper

½ teaspoon poultry seasoning

½ teaspoon paprika

½ teaspoon cayenne

¼ teaspoon dry mustard

1 (2½ to 3½ pound) frying chicken, cut up into 8 pieces

¼ cup all-purpose unbleached flour

2¼ teaspoons garlic salt

¼ to ½ teaspoon salt

¼ teaspoon celery salt

Lard, for frying

In a large bowl, combine the black pepper, poultry seasoning, paprika, cayenne, and dry mustard. Dredge the chicken pieces in the spices.

In a paper or plastic bag, combine the flour, garlic salt, salt, and celery salt; shake to mix. Add the chicken, a few pieces at a time, and shake to coat.

Heat the lard to 340°F and 2 inches deep in an electric skillet or on medium heat in a large cast-iron skillet. Add the chicken pieces and fry for 30 minutes, turning every 10 minutes. Increase the heat to 355°F for an electric skillet or medium-high for a regular skillet. Fry for an additional 5 minutes, or until the meat is no longer pink at the bone. Remove the chicken from the fat and drain on paper towels.

CHICKEN and DUMPLINGS

This very old-fashioned rendition of chicken and dumplings is probably the way your grandparents used to make it. Nothing extra has been added—no vegetables, no noodles—this really is just chicken and dumplings. Using a free-range organic bird is all you need to celebrate the true flavor of chicken. Add a teaspoon or two of your favorite dried herbs and a bay leaf to spice up the broth. Serves 6

1 (3- to 5-pound) broiler chicken, dressed and cut into 8 pieces

¼ teaspoon black pepper

2 teaspoons salt

2 cups all-purpose unbleached flour

4 teaspoons baking powder

2 tablespoons lard, cold and coarsely chopped

1 cup milk

In a large saucepan, place the chicken pieces; add enough water to cover. Add the pepper and 1 teaspoon salt. Cover and simmer until the chicken is tender, about 1 hour.

To prepare the dumplings, place the flour, baking powder, and the remaining 1 teaspoon salt in a large bowl. Using a pastry blender or fork, cut in the lard until the mixture resembles coarse crumbs. Add the milk, ¼ cup at a time, and mix until a soft dough forms; set aside.

Once the chicken is fully cooked and no longer pink at the bone, transfer it to a cutting board. Remove the skin, shred the chicken, and discard the bones. Return the meat to the pot. Bring the stew to a boil again, then drop the dough by teaspoonfuls into the pot. Cover the pot; boil the broth and dumplings for 12 minutes, until the dumplings have doubled in size. Serve immediately.

JAMBALAYA

Weeknight cooking begs for one-skillet meals, especially those utilizing leftover meat. Jambalaya is a spicy, tasty dish that fits the bill. Substitute beef, pork, or shrimp for the chicken if you prefer; if substituting shrimp (cooked or raw), add it during the last couple of minutes of cooking rather than at the beginning. Serve with a bottle of Tabasco for a spicy kick.   Serves 4

1 tablespoon lard

1 medium yellow onion, chopped

1 cup chopped celery

2 cloves garlic, minced

1 cup raw white rice

2 cups canned diced tomatoes

1 cup chopped cooked chicken

½ teaspoon salt

¼ teaspoon cayenne pepper (optional)

2 tablespoons chopped parsley

In a large skillet, heat the lard over medium heat. Add the onion, celery, garlic, and rice; sauté for 5 minutes.

Add the tomatoes, chicken, salt, and cayenne pepper, if using; heat to simmering. Reduce the heat to low, cover, and cook slowly, 35 to 45 minutes, stirring occasionally, until the rice is tender and the liquid has mostly evaporated.

Sprinkle the parsley over the dish and serve immediately.

SOUTHERN FRIED CHICKEN

Born in the South, this native recipe embodies southern hospitality and Sunday suppers after church. The key ingredient is buttermilk, which, along with other dairy products such as yogurt, tenderizes meat. The result is a crispier, juicier piece of fried chicken . . . finger-licking good!
Serves 4 to 6

1 cup all-purpose unbleached flour

½ teaspoon salt

½ teaspoon white pepper

2 cups buttermilk

Lard, for frying

1 frying chicken (2 to 2½ pounds), cut up into 8 pieces

Combine the flour, salt, and white pepper in a paper bag. Place the buttermilk in a large bowl. Set both aside.

In a heavy cast-iron skillet, heat the lard to 340°F and 1½ to 2 inches deep (start with 2 cups, adding more as needed). One by one, coat the chicken pieces in the buttermilk, then shake in the bag until well covered with the seasoned flour.

Add the chicken pieces to the hot fat, leaving a little space between the pieces so they're not crowded. Reduce the heat to medium and cook until the underside is golden brown, about 15 minutes. Turn and cook until the other side is brown. Reduce the heat to low; cover and cook an additional 10 minutes, or until the chicken is no longer pink at the bone. Remove the chicken from the fat and drain on paper towels.

HOMEMADE NOODLES with CHICKEN BROTH

You'll be delightfully surprised at how easy homemade noodles are to make. Whenever you have a bit of leftover chicken or turkey from a meal, toss it in some broth with these noodles and you'll have a simple, nourishing supper—perfect for a cold winter evening or for a child with the sniffles.   Serves 6

3 eggs

1 tablespoon water

1 tablespoon milk

½ teaspoon salt

1 tablespoon lard, melted and cooled

2 to 2¼ cups all-purpose unbleached flour

1 scant teaspoon baking powder

SOUP

2 quarts (8 cups) chicken or turkey broth

5 tablespoons all-purpose unbleached flour

1½ cups cooked and chopped chicken or turkey

1 teaspoon fresh or dried herbs of your choice

In a large bowl, combine the eggs, water, and milk. With an electric mixer, beat well on medium speed for 1 minute. Add the salt and lard; beat well.

In a separate bowl, whisk together 2 cups of flour and the baking powder. Add gradually to the egg mixture, beating on low speed. Switch to a rubber spatula and stir in more flour, up to ¼ cup if needed, to make a stiff dough.

Turn the dough onto a floured board and knead into a ball. Sprinkle more flour on the board and using a rolling pin, roll out the dough as thinly as possible, about ¹⁄₁₆ inch. Using a pizza wheel, slice the dough into strips ¼ inch wide, then slice again in half crosswise. Transfer the noodles to a wire rack and cover loosely with a lint-free cloth. Leave to dry for 2 hours.

To make a soup, place the broth in a stockpot and bring to a boil. Whisk in the flour to thicken. Add the poultry and the noodles, lower the heat to medium, and cook for 30 to 35 minutes, until the noodles are tender and the broth is thickened. Stir in the herbs. Serve immediately.

SPAGHETTI and CHICKEN LIVERS

Pasta alla Caruso—named after the great Italian tenor, Enrico Caruso—is a dish invented by Italians in America who found chicken to be a widely available commodity (not so in Italy until after World War II) and chicken livers at giveaway prices. It began appearing on the menus of Little Italy's restaurants sometime in the 1950s. Crisped in lard, the chicken livers provide creamy richness, the mushrooms, earthiness, and the tomato sauce, sweetness. Mangiare! Serves 8

2 (8-ounce) packages spaghetti

2 tablespoons olive oil

1 large yellow onion, diced

2 cups tomato juice

½ teaspoon salt

¼ teaspoon black pepper

½ cup grated mozzarella cheese

½ cup lard

½ pound fresh white button or shiitake mushrooms, rinsed, dried, and sliced

1 pound chicken livers, sliced into ½-inch pieces

¼ cup grated Parmesan cheese

In a large pot of boiling salted water, cook the spaghetti until tender; drain and set aside.

In a large skillet, heat the olive oil over medium-high heat. Add the onion and sauté for 10 minutes, until golden brown. Add the tomato juice, salt, and pepper; stir to mix. Add the mozzarella cheese gradually, blending thoroughly. Lower the heat and add the spaghetti; simmer for 10 minutes, stirring constantly, until thoroughly heated.

In a separate skillet, heat the lard over medium-high heat. Add the mushrooms and chicken livers and sauté for 10 minutes, until the mushrooms are browned and the livers are cooked through.

Place the spaghetti mixture on a serving platter; pour the sautéed livers and mushrooms over the top. Sprinkle with the Parmesan cheese and serve immediately.

EASTER HAM PIE

Another recipe born from necessity, Easter Ham Pie is really a quiche, and it makes good use of all that leftover traditional Easter ham. You'll end up with 4 pies on your hands afterward, so once they've cooled completely, wrap them tightly in plastic and freeze. They'll look awfully good in a few weeks or months and you'll pat yourself on the back for going to the trouble. Makes four 8-inch pies

CRUST

4 cups all-purpose unbleached flour

3 teaspoons baking powder

½ teaspoon salt

3 teaspoons sugar

½ cup lard, cold and coarsely chopped

9 eggs

½ cup to 1 cup milk

FILLING

3 cups diced ham

3 pounds ricotta cheese

1 cup grated Romano cheese

4 hard-boiled eggs, peeled and sliced

1 teaspoon milk

Salt and black pepper

Pinch of paprika

In a large bowl, combine the flour, baking powder, salt, and sugar. Using a pastry blender, cut in the lard until the mixture resembles coarse crumbs. Make a well in the center of the dry mixture; add 4 eggs and mix. Add the milk, ¼ cup at a time, and stir. Add just enough to make a fairly soft dough. Cut the dough into quarters.

Turn the dough onto a lightly floured board. Using a rolling pin, roll each quarter into a 14-inch crust and line four 8-inch pie pans, allowing for considerable overhang. Chill the crusts in the refrigerator while you prepare the filling.

Preheat the oven to 375°F.

In a large bowl, mix the ham, 4 beaten eggs, the cheeses, and egg slices. Divide the mixture evenly among the four crust-lined pans. Take the overhanging dough and fold it up over the filling; use cold water to seal where the crust overlaps. Beat the 1 remaining egg with the milk to make a wash. Brush the pie tops, including the filling, with the wash. Season with salt and pepper; sprinkle on paprika for color.

Bake for 40 to 45 minutes, until the crust is golden brown and the filling is set. (The filling will puff up, but it will settle when cooled.) Cool on wire racks. Serve warm or at room temperature, or freeze (see recipe introduction).

To bake after the pie has been frozen, defrost the pie in the refrigerator and bake as directed.

RAISING OUR OWN MEAT

We still raise and butcher our own meat, although we now take the animals to the local meat locker and they do the deed, because I am concerned about what we eat. By raising our own, I know what it has been fed and how it is handled, and that makes me especially happy when I hear about foodborne illnesses and meat recalls.

Lard, of course, is one of the products from the hog butchering, and the locker gladly saves the lard and even runs it through a grinder for me. I bring it home and render it in the oven, electric roaster, or on top of the stove, whichever method works at the time.

I would not dream of using anything else for pie crust. By putting lard into containers in the freezer, you do not have to worry about the lard becoming rancid. Lard purchased in the store has additives to help it remain fresh, but then again we have the issue of something added.

Any natural food has to be better than processed. The key is always moderation and a balanced diet.

Rose Anderson, Taunton, Minnesota

COUNTRY FRIED CHICKEN

Dredged in cornmeal instead of the traditional flour, this chicken is different in yet another way: It's finished in the oven after being browned in lard. If you'd rather focus on side dishes than hover over the fryer, this fried chicken recipe is the one for you. **Serves 4 to 6**

1 cup finely ground cornmeal

2 teaspoons salt

¼ teaspoon black pepper

1 frying chicken, cut into 8 pieces

½ cup lard

Preheat the oven to 350°F.

In a large bowl, combine the cornmeal, salt, and pepper; mix well. Dip the chicken pieces in the flour mixture; set aside.

In a large skillet, heat the lard to 350°F. Place the chicken in the hot fat and fry until browned, turning often, about 10 minutes. When browned, remove the chicken from the skillet and arrange in a 13 by 9-inch baking dish.

Bake for 35 to 40 minutes, until the chicken is no longer pink at the bone.

PORK CHOP SKILLET MEAL

Skillet meals are a godsend after a tiring day of work when you can't face a parade of pans and dishes. This fun, one-skillet meal also makes for an interesting presentation; bring the skillet straight to the table and serve. A simple loaf of crusty bread makes the perfect accompaniment.
Serves 4

4 tablespoons lard

4 pork chops, 1 inch thick

4 slices onion, ½ inch thick

4 rings green pepper, ½ inch thick

4 tablespoons raw rice

3 cups canned diced tomatoes

1 cup diced celery

In a large skillet, heat the lard over medium-high heat. Add the pork chops and sear on both sides.

Place 1 onion slice and 1 green pepper ring on each chop. Add 1 tablespoon of rice to the center of each ring. Pour the tomatoes around the chops and sprinkle the whole dish with the celery.

Reduce the heat to low, cover, and simmer for 1 hour, until the chops and rice are tender. Serve immediately.

PORK PIE

Pork pies are traditional English meat pies sealed in a pastry crust. This American version simplifies the process in order to get dinner on the table much more quickly—it has only a top crust, which can be pulled together in minutes. Filled with vegetables and gravy, this hearty fare deeply satisfies the appetite when the weather has turned chilly. Serve with a side salad or warm caraway sauerkraut. Serves 4 to 6

 1 pound pork roast

3 medium potatoes, peeled and diced

½ cup diced carrot

½ cup peas

½ cup green beans

½ cup diced celery

1 large yellow onion, diced

1½ cups all-purpose unbleached flour

3 teaspoons baking powder

1 teaspoon salt

¾ cup milk

2 tablespoons lard, cold and coarsely chopped

In a medium saucepan, simmer the pork for about 1 hour; transfer the meat to a dish and reserve the cooking liquid. When the pork has cooled to the touch, pull apart into small pieces and set aside.

Place the potatoes in a large saucepan and cover with water. Boil and cook for 10 minutes, then add the carrot, peas, green beans, celery, and onion; cook until tender, about 10 minutes. Reserve ½ cup of the cooking liquid.

In a small bowl, combine both of the reserved cooking liquids with 3 tablespoons of the flour; whisk together to make a gravy. Place the pork and vegetables in a 2-quart baking dish and pour the gravy over everything.

Preheat the oven to 450°F.

In a large bowl, combine the remaining flour, the baking powder, salt, and milk; stir together. Using a pastry blender, cut in the lard until the mixture resembles coarse crumbs, then gather up the mixture into a ball. Turn the dough onto a floured board and roll out to a diameter 1 inch larger than your baking dish. Place the crust over the ingredients in the dish and tuck in the edges so you have very little overhang.

Bake for 30 minutes, until the crust is golden brown.

SOME RECIPES MUST HAVE LARD I know of two recipes that must have lard in them to taste as they should. One is a French-Canadian dish I remember from my childhood, Soupe aux Pois, yellow pea soup. The other is the New Mexican state cookie, the biscochito, an anise seed–laced shortbread powdered with cinnamon sugar.

Heavenly, both of them, but not without lard!

Jane, via e-mail

BRITISH PASTIES

Pasties, similar to bierocks, are filled pocket pastries, though the difference is that British pasties (commonly known as Cornish pasties) call for uncooked filling before baking. Pasties came to America via the Cornish people who immigrated to Michigan's Upper Peninsula in the mid-nineteenth century to work in the mines. Miners carried pasties in their lunch pails and reheated them on shovels held over the candles worn on their hats. May 24 is Michigan Pasty Day, where the food is considered a regional specialty. Michiganians love to eat their pasties cold with ketchup. Serves 4

CRUST

¾ cup lard, frozen and finely grated, plus more for greasing the pan

3 cups all-purpose unbleached flour

1 teaspoon salt

Ice water

FILLING

½ pound ground pork

½ pound ground beef

2 cups finely sliced onions

1 cup finely sliced turnips

1 cup finely sliced potatoes

Salt and black pepper

Preheat the oven to 400°F. Grease a baking sheet with lard and set aside.

In a large bowl, combine the lard, flour, and salt. Using your fingers, mix together until it resembles fine crumbs. Add the ice water, ¼ cup at a time (up to about 1 cup total), and mix until the dough sticks together firmly.

Turn the dough onto a floured board. Using a rolling pin, roll out the dough to a ⅛-inch thickness and use an 8-inch pie plate, turned upside down, as a template to cut out 4 pasties.

In a large bowl, place all the filling ingredients; mix well. Distribute the filling evenly among the 4 pasties. Season to taste with salt and pepper. Bring up the sides of the pasty to meet in the middle; press together firmly and crimp with a fork or your fingers. Place the pasties on the prepared baking sheet and prick each one 3 times with a fork to vent.

Bake for 1 hour, until the pasties are golden brown and the filling is cooked through. Serve warm or cold.

BAKED TUNA

You might have turned up your nose when you saw the name of this recipe, but this updated retro classic is better than ever. And c'mon, who can resist the kitschy charm of a crushed-cornflakes topping? Serves 6

6 tablespoons lard, plus more
for greasing the dish

3 tablespoons flour

2 cups milk

1 (8-ounce) package egg noodles,
cooked and drained

1 cup flaked albacore tuna

1 cup frozen peas

2 roasted red peppers (jarred,
in water), chopped

¼ teaspoon crushed red pepper flakes

Salt and black pepper

1 cup crushed cornflakes

Preheat the oven to 375°F. Grease a
1½-quart casserole dish and set aside.

In a small saucepan, heat the lard over
medium heat. Add the flour gradually,
stirring constantly, until a paste is formed;
stir and cook for 3 minutes. Add the milk ¼
cup at a time, stirring constantly, allowing
the liquid to absorb after each addition;
simmer for 5 minutes and remove from the
heat.

In the prepared casserole dish, alternate
layers of noodles, tuna, peas, and red peppers,
covering each layer with sauce. Sprinkle on
the crushed red pepper flakes and season
to taste with salt and pepper. Spread the
cornflakes evenly over the casserole.

Bake for 35 to 40 minutes, until heated
through. Serve immediately.

FISH FILLETS CREOLE

If you've been meaning to eat more fish but just can't figure out how to do it easily, give this healthy and light recipe—which utilizes frozen fillets—a try. For variation, substitute frozen shrimp for the fillets. Serve with sautéed or grilled vegetables over rice for a Creole-style meal.
Serves 4

1 tablespoon lard, plus more for greasing the dish

1 green pepper, chopped

½ cup chopped onion

2 cups canned diced tomatoes

¼ teaspoon salt

⅛ teaspoon black pepper

¼ teaspoon Creole or Cajun seasoning

1 pound frozen fish fillets (halibut, tilapia, cod, or other white fish)

Preheat the oven to 350°F. Grease a 2-quart casserole dish and set aside.

In a large skillet, heat the lard over medium-high heat. Sauté the green pepper and onion in the lard until soft but not brown.

Add the tomatoes, salt, pepper, and Creole seasoning; simmer for 10 minutes.

Place the frozen fish in the prepared casserole dish. Pour the tomato mixture over the fish and bake for 30 minutes, until bubbling.

FOIL-BAKED FISH

The epitome of easy and delicious, foil-baked fish is poached in a simple liquid; a dot of lard is added to provide the necessary fat for the body to assimilate the nutrients in the fish. The vegetables will bubble and meld and create a stew upon which to serve the fish. Select any white fish (catfish, snapper, walleye, tilapia, sole, flounder) at the fishmonger's counter that looks fresh and suits your budget. **Serves 4**

4 fish fillets (12 ounces to 1 pound total)

4 teaspoons lard

Salt and black pepper

2 teaspoons paprika

1 large tomato, chopped

1 onion, chopped

½ green pepper, chopped

½ medium cucumber, peeled and chopped

2 tablespoons lemon juice

2 tablespoons chopped parsley

Preheat the oven to 350°F.

Tear off 2 large sheets of foil; place 2 fish fillets in the center of each sheet. Dot each fillet with 1 teaspoon of lard and season generously with salt, pepper, and ½ teaspoon of paprika.

Distribute the tomato, onion, green pepper, and cucumber evenly over the fillets and sprinkle with the lemon juice and parsley. Fold up the ends of the foil and seal the edges.

Place the foil packets in a shallow 13 by 9-inch baking dish and bake for 30 minutes, until the liquid is bubbling and the fish is opaque and cooked through. Serve immediately.

SALMON CROQUETTES

Croquette is just a fancy word for "patties" or "cakes," so the next time you want to impress folks, serve them this salmon version of crab cakes. If you've got a bit of leftover grilled or poached salmon—rather than the canned fish that's called for—these will taste even better. The rémoulade sauce complements the salmon perfectly, and the ingredients are so flexible that substitutions can be readily made: sour cream for mayonnaise, shallots for garlic, and so on. Serves 8

2 tablespoons butter

4 tablespoons all-purpose
unbleached flour

¾ teaspoon salt

Pinch of black pepper

1 cup milk

1 (16-ounce) can salmon,
without bones, flaked

2 tablespoons chopped parsley

½ teaspoon lemon juice

Lard, for frying

1 egg, slightly beaten

2 tablespoons water

¾ cup bread crumbs

RÉMOULADE

½ cup mayonnaise

½ teaspoon capers, drained and rinsed

½ teaspoon Dijon mustard

1 small clove garlic, chopped

1½ teaspoons chopped sweet pickle

1 teaspoon fresh lemon juice

1 teaspoon minced fresh chives

To make a white sauce, melt the butter in a saucepan over low heat. Add the flour, salt, and pepper; whisk together well and cook for 3 minutes. Add the milk slowly, whisking constantly, and continue cooking until the mixture thickens. Remove from the heat.

In a small bowl, combine the salmon with the parsley, lemon juice, and hot white sauce. Mix well and season with salt and pepper. Cover and refrigerate until firm.

In a large skillet, heat the lard over medium-high heat to ¼ inch deep.

In a small bowl, beat the egg with the water. Pour the bread crumbs onto a small plate. Using your hands, form the salmon into 8 equal-sized patties. Working in batches, dredge the patties in the bread crumbs, then dip into the egg mixture, then dredge again in the bread crumbs. Fry in hot fat for 2 to 3 minutes on each side, until golden brown. Drain on paper towels.

To prepare the rémoulade, place all the ingredients in a small bowl and whisk until smooth; refrigerate until served. Rémoulade can be made up to 3 days in advance.

HERITAGE BREEDS

HERITAGE BREEDS We raise heritage breed pigs and sell leaf fat and lard. We also use it ourselves, and it is fantastic! Best pies, sweet or meat! Best pastries, especially with leaf lard. And using it for frying creates the ultimate popcorn, fries, stir-fries, chicken, ribs, veggies, and anything else you would fry.

Here are some related Web sites we really like:

lardlovers.ning.com

www.lard.net

jacquelinechurch.com/pig-tales-a-fish-friends/1840-for-the-love-of-lard

Pride Sasser, Rock House Farm, Morganton, North Carolina
www.RockHouseFarm.info

CRAB CAKES

Enjoy the taste of the Maryland seashore, even when fresh crabmeat isn't an option. Whip up a homemade tartar sauce with mayonnaise and diced sweet pickles. Or for a lighter version, use equal parts sour cream and mayo, a pinch of minced shallots or onions, and some fresh aromatic herbs of your choice (cilantro, dill, basil, and tarragon are all delicious). **Serves 4**

1 (6.5-ounce) can crabmeat, drained

½ cup bread crumbs

1 egg, beaten

1 tablespoon Worcestershire sauce

1 tablespoon chopped green onion (white and green parts)

Salt and black pepper

Lard, for frying

In a large bowl, place the crabmeat, bread crumbs, egg, Worcestershire sauce, and onion. Season with salt and pepper; mix well. Shape into 4 equal-sized patties. (If more moisture is needed to form patties, add a dash of melted lard.)

In a large skillet, heat the lard over medium-high heat. Fry the patties 3 to 4 minutes on each side, until golden brown. Drain on paper towels and serve immediately.

POTATO LOAF

When you're in the mood for meat and potatoes but your larder is fresh out of the former, pull together this meatless loaf—flavored with onion, sage, and walnuts—that gets its bulk from potatoes. A delicious aroma will waft through the house as it bakes, luring diners to the table. Serve with an assortment of toppings, including butter, applesauce, sour cream, cheese, and chives. **Serves 8**

3 tablespoons lard, melted and cooled slightly, plus more for greasing the pan

5 large russet potatoes, peeled and cut into large chunks

1 large yellow onion, peeled and quartered

¾ cup walnuts

2 eggs, beaten

¾ teaspoon crumbled sage

1½ teaspoons salt

1 cup fine bread crumbs

Preheat the oven to 350°F. Grease a 9 by 5-inch loaf pan with lard and set aside.

Place half the potatoes, half the onion, and half the walnuts in the bowl of a food processor fitted with a metal blade. Pulse a few times to combine—the mixture should be very coarse; transfer to a large bowl. Repeat with the other half of the potatoes, onion, and walnuts.

Add the eggs, sage, lard, salt, and ¾ cup of the bread crumbs to the potato mixture and mix well. Place the mixture in the prepared loaf pan and pat down.

Bake for 30 minutes, then sprinkle the remaining ¼ cup of bread crumbs over the top of the loaf. Bake for an additional 15 minutes, until the loaf is heated through and the bread crumbs are toasted. Allow to cool for 10 minutes before slicing. Serve warm.

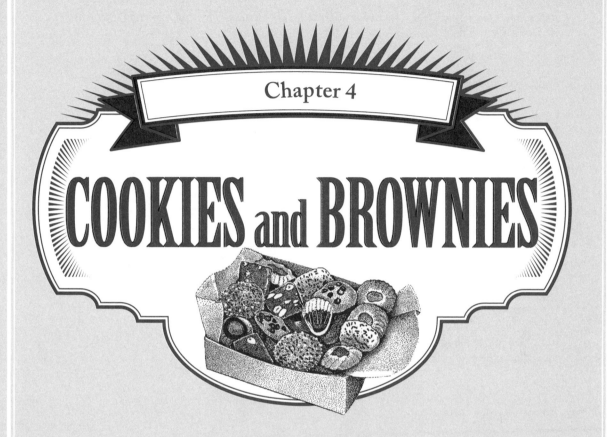

Chapter 4

COOKIES and BROWNIES

JUNE CLEAVER'S COOKIES

When Wally and the "Beav" got home from school, they always had some sort of school drama to unload on mom. June Cleaver knew her kids well and was prepared to tackle anything with a plate of their favorite cookies. This recipe will render the iconic cookies and milk your kids crave after school. Makes 5 dozen

1 cup lard, softened

1 cup granulated sugar

½ cup brown sugar, packed

2 eggs, beaten

2 teaspoons vanilla extract

2½ cups all-purpose unbleached flour

1 teaspoon salt

1 teaspoon baking soda

1 (12-ounce) package semisweet chocolate chips

Preheat the oven to 350°F.

In a large bowl, using an electric mixer on low speed, cream together the lard and sugars. Add the eggs and vanilla; beat until combined. Blend in the flour, salt, and baking soda; mix well. Stir in the chocolate chips.

Drop by rounded teaspoonfuls onto ungreased cookie sheets. Bake for 8 to 10 minutes, until golden brown and set. Cool on the sheets for 10 minutes, then transfer to wire racks to cool completely.

CHOCOLATE CHERRY CRUNCHES

These little balls of joy will remind you of Cella's classic chocolate-covered cherries. They're so special, you'll want to make a double batch at the holidays to give away in gift baskets or in a gift box at Valentine's Day. Forget the candy—give cookies! **Makes 2 dozen**

½ cup lard, softened, plus more
for greasing the pans

¾ cup confectioners' sugar

1 teaspoon vanilla extract

1 (1-ounce) square unsweetened
chocolate, melted

1½ cups all-purpose unbleached flour

⅛ teaspoon salt

24 maraschino cherries, well
drained, stems removed

Preheat the oven to 350°F. Grease two baking sheets with lard and set aside.

In a large bowl, cream together the lard and confectioners' sugar. Stir in the vanilla and melted chocolate. Add the flour and salt and mix until well combined.

Using a teaspoon, scoop out a heaping spoonful of dough; place a cherry in the middle, then place another heaping spoonful of dough on top. Roll the dough into a ball to encase the cherry securely. Repeat with the remaining dough and cherries.

Place the cookies on the prepared baking sheets and bake for 12 to 15 minutes, until the dough is set and lightly browned. Remove from the sheets and cool completely on wire racks.

WARTIME SUGAR COOKIES

Indicative of wartime baking, these sugar cookies contain a reduced amount of sugar and no butter. They're quite versatile, making them the perfect candidates for any kind of cookie cutter, frosting, or decoration, and they're sturdy and they travel well.   **Makes 5 dozen**

1 cup lard, softened, plus more for greasing the pans

½ cup sugar

2 eggs, beaten

½ cup light corn syrup

1 teaspoon vanilla extract

3½ cups sifted all-purpose unbleached flour

2 teaspoons baking powder

½ teaspoon salt

In a large bowl, cream the lard and sugar, using an electric mixer on low speed. Add the eggs, corn syrup, and vanilla; beat well.

In a separate bowl, sift together the flour, baking powder, and salt; add to the creamed mixture and stir well to form a ball. Cover with plastic wrap and chill for 2 hours.

Preheat the oven to 350°F. Grease two baking sheets with lard and set aside.

Turn the dough onto a floured board and flatten with the palm of your hand. Using a floured rolling pin, roll out to a ⅛-inch thickness. Use a cookie cutter to cut the dough, dipping in flour with each use; place the cookies 2 inches apart on the prepared baking sheets.

Bake for 10 minutes, until golden brown. Transfer the cookies to a wire rack to cool. Store in airtight containers for up to a week.

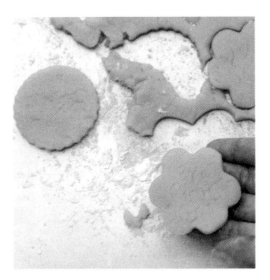

COCOA DROP COOKIES

This old-time recipe (edited for modern cooks) calls for sour milk, signaling that it may have been written prior to the availability of pasteurized milk in the early 1900s. Sour milk is different from "spoiled" milk in that it derives its sour taste naturally through bacterial fermentation at room temperature. Before rural electrification, raw milk would sour within two days in the "icebox." Sour milk can be made by adding lemon juice or vinegar to buttermilk, but homemade (live) yogurt is a better replacement. Even simpler, substitute store-bought buttermilk.
Makes 2 dozen

¾ cup lard, melted, plus more for greasing the pans

1½ cups sugar

½ cup cocoa

1 egg, well beaten

½ teaspoon baking soda

¼ teaspoon cream of tartar

¾ cup sour milk

1 cup chopped nuts of your choice

2 teaspoons vanilla extract

1 to 1½ cups all-purpose unbleached flour

Preheat the oven to 350°F. Grease two baking sheets with lard and set aside.

In a large bowl, using a wooden spoon, cream together the sugar, cocoa, and melted lard. Mix in the egg. Dissolve the baking soda and cream of tartar in the sour milk (or buttermilk). Add to the creamed mixture with the nuts and vanilla.

Mix in enough flour to make the right consistency to drop the dough from a teaspoon and retain its shape (start with 1 cup). Place on the prepared baking sheets.

Bake until the cookies are set, 8 to 10 minutes. Cool on sheets for 5 minutes, then transfer to a wire rack to cool completely.

THE AHA! INGREDIENT

At the beginning of my career as a journalist, I moved to New Mexico from Oklahoma in early spring and immediately fell in love with the place—the mountains, the vistas, the slow pace of life—and most of all, the food. I have always been a slave to flavor, and I had a reputation in my family as one who viewed the kitchen as much as a laboratory as a repository of tradition.

A new world of food opened up to me when I arrived in New Mexico, and of course, I immediately went to work trying to duplicate some of the dishes I had discovered. Green chile/chicken enchiladas weren't terribly difficult, nor was the delicious posole that one found at any community gathering. I had trouble figuring out the combination for red chili, however, and was astonished to discover that it had *no* tomatoes in it. Brought up all my life on the Tex-Mex version of chili, I couldn't believe that the red in New Mexico's chili came from dried peppers.

I remember clearly the first time I tasted my first real tamale. I had eaten only canned tamales up to that point and found them to be big gobs of mush. Then at an outdoor fair one summer afternoon in Albuquerque, I smelled something delicious in the air, followed the scent, and ended up buying some fresh homemade tamales. Holy Toledo, was that delicious.

I never tried to make tamales—they looked messy and complicated. But at Christmastime when I had another Holy Toledo moment, I did try to make the little seasonal cookies known as *bizcochitos* and just couldn't get them right. As it turns out, they shared a secret ingredient with the tamales.

I finally confessed to one of the Hispanic women I worked with that my *bizcochitos* tasted OK, but didn't come even close to hers for flavor and crispiness. She leaned in and whispered in my ear, cute and conspiratorial, that the secret was . . . *lard*—no Crisco, no butter, just good old-fashioned lard.

I was in my culinary snob period at the time, so I'm sure I recoiled noticeably. However, I went home, tried it, and instantly became a convert. In time, I learned that the only tamales worth eating were those made with lard, too. This was the beginning of the end of my culinary snob days. When I found out that the Hispanic women's unbeatable chicken enchiladas always included a can of Campbell's cream of chicken soup, my transformation was complete.

K. C. Compton, GRIT Executive Editor, Lawrence, Kansas

MINCEMEAT DROP COOKIES

True mincemeat always contains meat (beef, beef suet, or venison), but modern variations consist of chopped dried fruit, spices, and distilled spirits, making mincemeat less of a savory food and more of a sweet pie filling or other dessert. In New England, mincemeat pies are a traditional part of the Thanksgiving feast, served with a slice of cheddar cheese. Try these chewy, old-fashioned cookies, using commercially prepared mincemeat—or homemade mincemeat if you should be that lucky. Makes 2½ dozen

¼ cup lard, softened, plus more
for greasing the pans

1 cup mincemeat

½ cup sugar

1 egg, lightly beaten

1½ cups all-purpose unbleached flour

1 teaspoon baking powder

¼ teaspoon baking soda

½ teaspoon cinnamon

Pinch of salt

Chopped nuts of your choice (optional)

Preheat the oven to 350°F. Grease two baking sheets with lard and set aside.

In a large bowl, using a wooden spoon, cream together the mincemeat, sugar, and lard; stir in the egg. In a separate bowl, sift together the flour, baking powder, baking soda, cinnamon, and salt; add to the creamed mixture and blend well. Add the nuts, if using, and mix well.

Using a tablespoon, drop the dough onto the prepared baking sheets, 2 inches apart.

Bake for 14 to 16 minutes, until the edges are golden brown. Cool on sheets for 5 minutes, then transfer to wire racks to cool completely.

RAISIN-FILLED COOKIES

These delightful little raisin biscuits are based on the ancient fig roll pastry—preserved fruit wrapped in dough. Think of them as your handmade version of Fig Newtons. Until the late 1800s, a doctor's common diagnosis for most illnesses was "digestion problems," to which the treatment was daily intake of biscuits and fruit. Handmade and locally produced, fig rolls were the ideal solution to the problem. Serve these hunger-satisfying cookies with afternoon tea or coffee; they'll tide you over until supper. **Makes 2 dozen**

3 cups sugar

¾ cup lard, softened, plus more for greasing the pans

½ teaspoon salt

3 eggs

2 teaspoons vanilla extract

1 teaspoon baking soda dissolved in 1 teaspoon vinegar

1 cup milk

3 teaspoons baking powder

2 to 3 cups all-purpose unbleached flour

1 pound raisins

1 cup water

In a large bowl, using a wooden spoon, cream together 2 scant cups sugar, the lard, and salt until fluffy. Add 2 eggs, 1 teaspoon of vanilla, the dissolved baking soda, milk, baking powder, and enough flour to make the dough stick together in a ball. Cut the dough in half and press each half into a disk. Wrap each disk tightly in plastic and refrigerate overnight.

Preheat the oven to 350°F. Remove the dough from the refrigerator and let stand while you prepare the filling. Grease two baking sheets with lard and set aside.

To prepare the filling, place the raisins in the bowl of a food processor fitted with a metal blade; grind to a coarse paste. Combine the raisins, the remaining 1 cup of sugar, and the water in a saucepan over low heat; cook for 5 minutes. Add 2 tablespoons of flour and whisk to thicken; cook for 3 minutes. Remove from the heat and stir in the remaining 1 teaspoon of vanilla; set aside to cool.

Turn the dough onto a lightly floured surface. Using a floured rolling pin, roll the dough to a ¼-inch thickness. Use a 2½-inch round cookie or biscuit cutter dipped in sugar to cut out the cookies. Transfer the dough rounds to the prepared baking sheets.

Place about 1 tablespoon of the raisin mixture in the center of each dough round; cover with another dough round. Press or crimp together the edges to seal the filling inside.

In a small bowl, beat the remaining egg until frothy. Using a pastry brush, paint each cookie with the beaten egg.

Bake for 10 minutes, until the cookies are golden brown and doubled in size. Cool on the baking sheets for 10 minutes, then transfer to wire racks to cool completely.

MICROWAVE TO RENDER LARD

Many people do not like to render lard because it takes a long time and smells up the kitchen. Somewhere in my travels I received an easy recipe for rendering lard and have been using it for years. We raise our own pigs, so we always have the fat available, but I'm sure any butcher shop could supply the fat.

Cut the fat in small pieces and put them in a flat-bottomed glass dish. Microwave for 10 to 12 minutes. Pour the hot lard through a strainer into glass canning jars. Put the caps on and you are done!

The cracklings are what you strain out. Some people like to eat them, but I find them too "fatty." We use the lard for pies, deep-frying, and anything else that calls for shortening.

Kathy Bednarski, Florence, Wisconsin

SCHOOL DAY COOKIES

These healthier cookies will be devoured by kids of all ages. The dates, walnuts, and oats provide nutrition in the form of fiber, fat, and complex carbohydrates, respectively, which will help fuel their bodies and minds while doin' readin', writin', and 'rithmetic. And better still, they won't come home feeling ravenous and bedraggled. Pack these cookies in the freezer and dole them out all month in lunch boxes.   Makes 4 dozen

1 cup lard, softened, plus more for greasing the pans

1 cup sugar

2 eggs, beaten

¼ cup fresh orange juice

2 tablespoons grated orange zest

1 teaspoon vanilla extract

2 cups all-purpose unbleached flour

½ teaspoon salt

1 teaspoon baking soda

2 cups quick-cooking oats

½ cup chopped dates

½ cup chopped walnuts

Preheat the oven to 375°F. Grease two baking sheets with lard and set aside.

In a large bowl, using an electric hand mixer on low speed, cream together the lard and sugar thoroughly. Add the eggs and beat well. Add the orange juice, zest, and vanilla.

In a separate bowl, sift together the flour, salt, and baking soda; mix into the creamed mixture. Stir in the oats, dates, and walnuts.

Using a teaspoon, drop by the spoonful onto the prepared baking sheets, 2 inches apart. Bake for 12 to 15 minutes, until the tops are set and the edges are golden brown. Transfer the cookies to wire racks to cool completely.

LEMON NUT REFRIGERATOR COOKIES

Refrigerator cookies, also known as icebox cookies, are made from a stiff dough that stiffens further when refrigerated. The dough is shaped into rolls, then sliced into round cookies before baking. If you love the convenience of those cookie dough cylinders sold in the refrigerated aisle of the supermarket, make your own version, devoid of ingredients you can't pronounce. You can refrigerate the dough for a week to 10 days, and you can freeze the cookies. **Makes 7 dozen**

1 cup lard, softened

½ cup granulated sugar

½ cup brown sugar, packed

2 tablespoons lemon juice

1 egg

2½ cups all-purpose unbleached flour

½ teaspoon salt

¼ teaspoon baking soda

1 tablespoon grated lemon zest

½ cup chopped nuts of your choice

In a large bowl, cream together the lard and sugars using an electric mixer on low speed. Add the lemon juice and egg; beat well.

In a separate bowl, sift together the flour, salt, and baking soda; add to the creamed mixture and beat until well combined. Stir in the lemon zest and nuts.

Divide the dough in half and roll into logs about 2 inches in diameter. Wrap the roll first in wax paper, then in plastic. Chill thoroughly in the refrigerator.

To bake the cookies, preheat the oven to 400°F. Cut the log into ⅛-inch slices and place on ungreased baking sheets. Bake for 10 minutes, until the cookies are set and the edges are golden brown.

COCONUT ISLAND COOKIES

These little tropical mounds—dark chocolate–coconut cookies with a hint of coffee, covered in a shiny chocolate icing and topped with an ethereal mound of white coconut—are a sight to behold and heavenly to taste. You won't be able to stop at just one. Makes 3½ dozen

½ cup lard, softened, plus more
for greasing the pans

2 cups all-purpose unbleached flour, sifted

½ teaspoon salt

½ teaspoon baking soda

3 (1-ounce) squares
unsweetened chocolate

¼ cup hot coffee

1 cup brown sugar, packed

1 egg

⅔ cup sour cream

1 cup finely shredded
unsweetened coconut

ICING

1 (1-ounce) square
unsweetened chocolate

1 tablespoon plus 1
teaspoon salted butter

1 cup confectioners' sugar

2 tablespoons half-and-half

Preheat the oven to 375°F. Grease two baking sheets with lard and set aside.

In a medium bowl, sift together the flour, salt, and baking soda. Set aside.

In a saucepan over low heat, combine the chocolate and hot coffee; heat until the chocolate is melted, stirring frequently. Remove from the heat and let cool.

In a large bowl, cream the lard with the brown sugar, using an electric mixer on low speed. Blend in the egg and cooled chocolate mixture. Alternately, add the sifted mixture and the sour cream to the creamed mixture, beating well after each addition. Stir in ⅓ cup coconut.

Using a teaspoon, drop the dough by heaping spoonfuls onto the prepared baking sheets.

Bake for 12 to 15 minutes, until set. Cool the cookies on the baking sheets for 5 minutes, then transfer to a wire rack to cool completely.

Meanwhile, prepare the icing: Melt together the chocolate and butter in a small saucepan over low heat. Whisk in a third of the confectioners' sugar, then 1 tablespoon of half-and-half, then continue adding the remaining confectioners' sugar and half-and-half, whisking until smooth. The icing will be somewhere between a thick glaze and a thin frosting.

While the cookies are still warm, drop a dollop of icing on each cookie and sprinkle the tops with the remaining ⅔ cup of coconut. Cool completely, then store in a single layer in a tightly covered container.

PFEFFERNÜSSE (PEPPERNUT COOKIES)

Pfeffernüsse, which translates to "pepper nuts," is a traditional German spiced Christmas cookie with a sweet, peppery flavor. As with most ancient recipes, endless variations exist—some with pepper, some without; some with nuts, some just . . . hard as nuts. Pfeffernüsse are extremely hard when first baked, though they mellow and soften with age. Serve with coffee, tea, or milk for dunking. This recipe will make plenty of cookies with which to spread holiday cheer. **Makes 6 to 8 dozen**

2 cups molasses

2 cups honey

1 pound brown sugar

1 cup unsalted butter

1 cup lard

1 teaspoon freshly ground black pepper

1 teaspoon ground cloves

1 teaspoon allspice

2½ teaspoons cinnamon

3 teaspoons ground anise

½ teaspoon salt

3 eggs, well beaten

16 cups sifted all-purpose unbleached flour

2 tablespoons baking powder

1 teaspoon baking soda

2 cups confectioners' sugar

In a large saucepan, combine the molasses, honey, brown sugar, butter, and lard; heat gently until melted together. Remove from the heat and let cool slightly. Stir in the pepper, cloves, allspice, cinnamon, anise, salt, and eggs.

Sift together the sifted flour, baking powder, and baking soda. Gradually stir into the molasses mixture until moistened. Cover with plastic wrap and let stand overnight.

Preheat the oven to 375°F.

Roll the dough into balls about 1 inch in diameter and place 1 inch apart on ungreased baking sheets. Bake for 12 to 15 minutes, until set.

Place the confectioners' sugar in a paper bag. Working in batches, place several cookies in the bag and shake to coat. Store in airtight cookie tins with a slice of fresh apple or half an orange peel to prevent them from hardening (use more for larger containers). Leave to ripen and mellow for 2 to 3 weeks; then remove the apple or orange peel and store in an airtight jar. The cookies will keep for up to 8 weeks, but they won't last that long! Freeze for longer storage.

GRANDMA'S ICEBOX COOKIES

Grandma Stover's house was a welcoming place for kids to stop after school because she always had a roll of her famous icebox cookies in the refrigerator and she needed no excuse to bake. She'd slice off two cookies per kid (three for her grandkids), and they'd be ready to eat in just under 15 minutes.   Makes 5 dozen

1 cup brown sugar, packed

1 cup granulated sugar

½ cup unsalted butter, softened

½ cup lard, softened, plus more for greasing the pan

3 eggs

4½ cups all-purpose unbleached flour

1½ teaspoons baking soda

½ teaspoon salt

1 teaspoon cinnamon

1 cup finely chopped nuts of your choice

In a large bowl, using an electric mixer on low speed, cream together the sugars, butter, and lard until light and fluffy. Add the eggs, one at a time, beating well after each addition; set aside.

In a separate bowl, sift the flour, baking soda, salt, and cinnamon; add to the creamed mixture and beat until well combined. Stir in the nuts. With lightly floured hands, divide the dough in half. Shape each half into a 2-inch-diameter log. Wrap each log in wax paper, followed by plastic, and freeze overnight.

To bake the cookies: Preheat the oven to 350°F. Remove the dough from the refrigerator and thaw while the oven is heating. Grease 2 baking sheets with lard.

Slice the logs into ¼-inch-thick slices and bake for 10 to 12 minutes, until the cookies are set and the edges are just golden brown. Transfer to wire racks to cool.

YAM DROPS

Believe it or not, yams and sweet potatoes are botanically unrelated, though the two terms have been used interchangeably since the 1940s when sweet potato growers in Louisiana decided that labeling their crop "Louisiana Yams" had a certain panache. All "yams" marketed in the United States are actually sweet potatoes, as the true yam is not grown or sold anywhere stateside. These cookies represent a fine solution to leftover "yams" from your holiday meal. Makes 6 dozen

¾ cup lard, softened, plus more for greasing the pans

¼ cup salted butter

1½ cups brown sugar, packed

2 eggs, beaten

1 tablespoon fresh lemon juice

1 teaspoon vanilla extract

1 cup buttermilk

2 cups sifted all-purpose unbleached flour

2 teaspoons baking powder

1 teaspoon baking soda

¼ teaspoon salt

1½ cups mashed sweet potatoes

¼ cup chopped pecans

GLAZE

2 tablespoons plus 2 teaspoons salted butter, melted

1 to 1¼ cups confectioners' sugar

2 tablespoons fresh lemon juice

¼ teaspoon grated lemon zest

Preheat the oven to 350°F. Grease two baking sheets with lard and set aside.

In a large bowl, using an electric mixer on low speed, cream together the lard, butter, and brown sugar until fluffy; beat in the eggs, lemon juice, vanilla, and buttermilk.

In a separate bowl, combine the flour, baking powder, baking soda, and salt. Add the dry ingredients to the creamed mixture and blend well. Fold in the sweet potatoes and nuts.

Using a teaspoon, drop by spoonfuls onto the prepared baking sheets. Bake for 15 minutes, until the cookie edges are lightly browned. Transfer to a wire rack to cool.

To prepare the glaze, combine all the ingredients in a small bowl and whisk thoroughly, adding more lemon juice, water, or sugar to achieve the consistency of a thin paste. Using a teaspoon, drop a dollop of glaze over each cookie.

HOW HEALTHY IS PROCESSED? Growing up on a farm, we raised our own meat, including pigs. We used the fat and rendered our own lard. That is all we used.

I didn't have a special recipe for anything because whenever a recipe called for shortening, I used lard.

Being on my own without a family and reading the back of a shortening can, I discovered there is a lot of stuff added to the can. How healthy is that?

Lately I have been searching for a producer so I can get pig fat and render my own lard.

Barb Malikowski, Foley, Minnesota

WORLD WAR II HONEY COOKIES

During World War II, lots of common pantry staples were rationed, including butter, eggs, and sugar. As a result, a whole generation of bakers learned to do without and make appropriate substitutions where they could (see World War II Cake, page 186). This recipe replaces half the sugar with honey, reflecting the creator's make-do attitude of the time. As an added benefit of this substitution, honey extends the shelf life of these cookies due to its antibacterial properties.
Makes 16

½ cup lard, softened, plus
more for greasing the pan

½ cup sugar

½ cup honey

1 egg

1 teaspoon vanilla extract

⅔ cup all-purpose unbleached flour

½ teaspoon baking powder

½ teaspoon baking soda

¼ teaspoon salt

1 cup old-fashioned oats

1 cup unsweetened flaked coconut

½ cup chopped nuts of your choice

Preheat the oven to 350°F. Lightly grease a 13 by 9-inch baking pan with lard and set aside.

In a large bowl, combine the lard, sugar, and honey; mix well. Add the egg and vanilla; mix well and set aside.

In a separate bowl, sift together the flour, baking powder, baking soda, and salt. Add the sifted ingredients to the honey mixture and stir just until combined. Fold in the oats, coconut, and nuts.

Pour the batter into the prepared pan. Bake for 25 to 35 minutes, until the top is light golden brown and the center is set. Cool completely on wire racks and cut into squares or bars.

PRALINE COOKIES

Pralines, a specialty of New Orleans and the South, originated with French settlers in Louisiana who found abundant sugarcane and pecan trees. Praline recipes are a many splendored thing with countless recipes, formulations, and textures, but they're all basically the melding of burnt sugar and crunchy nuts. Burnt-sugar flavoring is available online through candy and spice suppliers.   Makes 8 dozen

⅔ cup lard, softened, plus more for greasing the pans

1¾ cups all-purpose unbleached flour, plus more for dusting the pans

1 cup sugar

½ cup mild molasses

2 eggs

½ teaspoon vanilla extract

1 teaspoon burnt sugar flavoring

½ teaspoon baking soda

¼ teaspoon ground mace

¼ teaspoon salt

1½ to 2 cups chopped pecans

Preheat the oven to 375°F. Grease two baking sheets with lard; dust lightly with flour and set aside.

In a saucepan over low heat, slowly melt the lard; remove from the heat and let cool. Transfer the melted lard to a large bowl. Add the sugar and molasses and stir well. Add the eggs, vanilla, and burnt sugar flavoring and mix well.

In a large bowl, sift together the flour, baking soda, mace, and salt ; add to the molasses mixture, mixing well. Stir in the nuts.

Drop by scant teaspoonfuls onto the prepared baking sheets, 2 inches apart. Bake for 8 to 10 minutes, until golden brown. Immediately transfer the cookies to wire racks to cool.

AMISH OATMEAL COOKIES

When the Amish people settled in America, they gravitated to rural areas where wheat, rye, corn, and barley flourished. As a result, grain products such as bread, cornmeal, and oatmeal became staples of their diet. They don't eat processed food, sticking mainly to products produced on their own farms. Amish women are prolific bakers and they take their baked goods seriously. This recipe reflects their food philosophy and is an interesting take on the usual oatmeal cookie. Makes 5 dozen

1½ cups raisins

1 cup peanuts

6 cups all-purpose unbleached flour

2 tablespoons baking powder

1 teaspoon nutmeg

1 teaspoon cinnamon

1 teaspoon salt

1½ cups lard, cold and coarsely chopped, plus more for greasing the pans

3 cups sugar

2½ cups old-fashioned oats

2 tablespoons baking soda

1 cup buttermilk

½ cup dark molasses

5 eggs

Combine the raisins and peanuts in the bowl of a food processor fitted with a metal blade; grind coarsely. Set aside.

In a very large bowl, sift together the flour, baking powder, nutmeg, cinnamon, and salt. Using a pastry blender, cut in the lard until the mixture resembles coarse crumbs. Stir in the sugar, oats, and raisin mixture, mixing well.

Dissolve the baking soda in the buttermilk; add to the dough and mix. Add the molasses and 3 beaten eggs, stirring well to combine. Cover the dough with plastic wrap and chill for 1 hour.

Preheat the oven to 375°F. Grease two baking sheets with lard and set aside.

Using your hands, roll the dough into walnut-sized balls and place on the prepared baking sheets. Using a spatula, press down on the balls to flatten slightly.

In a small bowl, beat the remaining 2 eggs and brush on each cookie. Bake for 10 to 12 minutes, until golden brown. Transfer the cookies to wire racks to cool.

PEANUT BUTTER COOKIES

Chewy, nutty, and sporting that telltale crosshatch pattern, these peanut butter cookies are what you remember eating at grandma's house. And they even take advantage of her secret ingredient—instant pudding. Use either creamy or crunchy peanut butter for variation. Serve with a tall glass of milk, of course. Makes 2½ dozen

⅓ cup lard, softened, plus more
for greasing the pans

1 cup all-purpose unbleached flour

½ teaspoon baking soda

⅛ teaspoon salt

½ cup creamy or chunky peanut butter

1 (4-serving-size) package
instant vanilla pudding mix

1 egg

Preheat the oven to 375°F. Grease two baking sheets with lard and set aside.

In a medium bowl, whisk together the flour, baking soda, and salt; set aside.

In a large bowl, using an electric mixer on low speed, cream the lard; blend in the peanut butter and pudding mix. Add the egg and beat until light and fluffy. Gradually add the flour mixture, beating well after each addition, until the dough is smooth.

Roll the dough into small balls and place on the prepared baking sheets. Using a fork, flatten each cookie; turn the fork 90 degrees and repeat, creating a crosshatch pattern.

Bake for 10 to 12 minutes, until lightly browned. Transfer to wire racks to cool completely.

ZOOKIES

Endless oddball recipes have been created as the result of prolific squash plants—and this is another one. Delicious and nutritious Zookies are a good way to use the scores of zucchini from your garden. So next summer, instead of sneaking bags of zucchini into your friends' and neighbors' unlocked cars, present them with bags of Zookies. They'll be pleasantly surprised.
Makes 4 dozen

½ cup lard, softened, plus more for greasing the pans

1 cup brown sugar, packed

1 egg

1 teaspoon grated orange zest

¾ teaspoon cinnamon

¼ teaspoon nutmeg

¼ teaspoon cloves

½ teaspoon salt

1¾ to 2 cups all-purpose unbleached flour

2 teaspoons baking powder

¼ cup milk

1 teaspoon vanilla extract

1½ cups shredded unpeeled zucchini

½ cup raisins

½ cup chopped pecans

Preheat the oven to 375°F. Lightly grease two baking sheets with lard and set aside.

In a large bowl, using an electric mixer on low speed, cream the lard; add the brown sugar and beat until fluffy. Add the egg, orange zest, cinnamon, nutmeg, cloves, and salt, mixing well to combine. In a small bowl, combine the flour and baking powder. Alternately add the flour mixture and the milk to the creamed mixture, beating well after each addition. Fold in the vanilla, zucchini, raisins, and pecans.

Using a tablespoon, drop by the spoonful onto the prepared baking sheets. Bake for 12 to 15 minutes, until golden brown. Cool for 5 minutes on the sheets, then transfer to wire racks to cool completely.

BIZCOCHITOS

In 1989, New Mexico deemed the bizcochito its official state cookie, making it the first state to have an official cookie. Seldom known outside of Hispanic cultures, bizcochitos are spicy, anise-flavored cookies served for special occasions such as weddings, baptisms, and especially Christmas. New Mexico chose bizcochitos in an effort to preserve traditional home baking and cookery. Serve with coffee on Christmas morning.   Makes 2 to 3 dozen, depending on size/shape of cutter

2 cups lard, softened, plus more for greasing the pans

1½ cups sugar

1½ teaspoons anise seeds

2 eggs, well beaten

6 cups sifted all-purpose unbleached flour

3 teaspoons baking powder

1 teaspoon salt

¼ cup water or brandy

1 teaspoon cinnamon

Preheat the oven to 375°F. Grease two baking sheets with lard and set aside.

In a large bowl, using an electric mixer on low speed, cream together the lard and 1 cup sugar; add the anise seeds and mix. Beat in the eggs until light and fluffy.

In a very large bowl, sift the sifted flour with the baking powder and salt; add to the creamed mixture and beat until well combined. Add the water or brandy and knead until well mixed.

Turn the dough onto a lightly floured surface. Using a floured rolling pin, roll the dough to a ½-inch thickness and cut into circles or fancy shapes (the fleur-de-lis shape is traditional).

Place the remaining ½ cup of sugar and the cinnamon in a small bowl; mix to combine. Roll the top of each cookie in the sugar mixture and place on the prepared baking sheets.

Bake for 15 minutes, until lightly browned. Transfer the cookies to wire racks to cool completely.

CHOCOLATE CARAMEL SWIRL BARS

There's a reason so many candy bars and sweet confections are based on the solid combination of chocolate and caramel—it's simply divine. Look for the bagged caramels that are sold sans wrappers for a time-saving bonus on this classic. Makes 16

⅔ cup lard, softened, plus
more for greasing the pan

1½ cups light brown sugar, packed

2 tablespoons water

1 teaspoon vanilla extract

2 eggs

1½ cups all-purpose unbleached flour

⅓ cup unsweetened cocoa

½ teaspoon salt

¼ teaspoon baking soda

1 (14-ounce) bag caramels
(40 to 45 pieces)

1 cup semisweet chocolate chips

Preheat the oven to 350°F. Grease a 13 by 9-inch baking pan with lard; set aside.

In a large bowl, cream the lard and sugar with 1 tablespoon of water and the vanilla, using an electric mixer on medium speed. Beat in the eggs.

In a separate bowl, whisk together the flour, cocoa, salt, and baking soda. Mix into the creamed mixture at low speed just until blended.

Place the caramels and the remaining 1 tablespoon of water in a microwave-safe bowl. Heat in the microwave on full power for 2 minutes; stir. Heat an additional minute if the caramels are not fully melted.

Spread half the cocoa mixture in the prepared pan. Using a rubber spatula, gently spread the caramel evenly over the cocoa mixture. Sprinkle the chocolate chips evenly over the top. Cover with the remaining cocoa mixture.

Bake for 25 to 30 minutes, or until a toothpick inserted in the center comes out clean. Cool in the pan on a wire rack. Cut into bars.

Fiesta Beef Potpie, page 74

Henrietta's Spicy Fried Chicken, page 86

**Homemade Noodles with
Chicken Broth, page 90**

Crab Cakes, page 104

Wartime Sugar Cookies, page 110

Pfeffernüsse (Peppernut Cookies), page 120

Applesauce Brownies, page 134

Spicy Pumpkin Bars
with Cream Cheese Icing, page 138

CALICO SQUARES

You've seen (or eaten) the everything bagel . . . well, here is the everything cookie. Calico Squares are so named to reflect their virtual calico quilt of flavors and textures. Many recipe variations exist, including those with almonds, oats, chocolate chips, white chocolate chips, dried cranberries, or anything else you've got in the pantry to contribute to the making of this soft oatmeal cookie. Have fun creating your own combinations. Makes 12

½ cup lard, plus more for greasing the pan

1 cup chopped black walnuts

1 cup chopped maraschino or candied cherries

½ cup raisins

2 eggs, slightly beaten

1 tablespoon granulated sugar

1 tablespoon grated orange zest

1⅓ cups all-purpose unbleached flour

½ teaspoon baking soda

⅛ teaspoon salt

1 (6-ounce) package butterscotch chips

½ cup brown sugar, packed

Preheat the oven to 350°F. Grease a 13 by 9 by 2-inch pan with lard and set aside.

In a medium bowl, combine the walnuts, cherries, raisins, eggs, granulated sugar, and orange zest; set aside.

In a separate bowl, sift together the flour, baking soda, and salt; set aside.

In a double boiler over hot water, melt together the butterscotch chips and lard, stirring frequently; remove from the heat and beat in the brown sugar. Stir in the sifted ingredients and mix well.

Spread the batter in the prepared pan and bake for 15 minutes. Remove from the oven and cover with the reserved walnut mixture. Return to the oven and bake for an additional 20 minutes. Cool completely on a wire rack and then cut into squares.

COFFEE BARS

This old-fashioned country favorite will soon be your favorite, too. Back in the day, coffee was expensive, so it was reserved for the hard-working adults of the household. With that in mind, a frosted coffee-flavored snack bar was something that tickled the hearts, and taste buds, of rural folks when presented with one.   Makes 2 dozen

1 cup lard, softened, plus more
for greasing the pans

1 cup brown sugar, packed

1 cup granulated sugar

3 eggs

3 cups sifted all-purpose
unbleached flour

1 teaspoon cinnamon

½ teaspoon ginger

½ teaspoon nutmeg

1 teaspoon baking powder

1 teaspoon baking soda

½ teaspoon salt

1 cup strong coffee, cold

1 teaspoon vanilla extract

½ cup chopped nuts of your choice

ICING

4 tablespoons salted butter

¼ cup hot coffee

2 cups confectioners' sugar

Pinch of salt

½ teaspoon vanilla extract

Preheat the oven to 325°F. Grease two 13 by 9-inch pans with lard and set aside.

In a large bowl, using an electric mixer on low speed, cream together the sugars and lard; add the eggs and beat until fluffy.

In a separate bowl, sift together the flour, cinnamon, ginger, nutmeg, baking powder, baking soda, and salt.

Alternately add the flour mixture and cold coffee to the creamed mixture, starting and ending with the flour mixture, beating well after each addition. Stir in the vanilla and nuts. Divide the mixture evenly between the two prepared pans.

Bake for 25 to 30 minutes, until a toothpick inserted in the center comes out clean. Cool on a wire rack.

To prepare the icing, combine the butter and hot coffee in a medium bowl. Add the confectioners' sugar, salt, and vanilla; whisk until smooth. Using an offset spatula, divide and spread the icing evenly between the two pans. Cut each pan into 12 bars.

RETHINKING STANCE Yes, my mother and grandmother—in Wooster, Ohio—both used lard for pie crusts and said nothing else would make such a flaky crust. They also used lard in gingerbread cookies. But as I grew up and saw that lard had such a bad rap, I ended up not using it. I never could make decent pie crusts, so I just buy commercial ones if I ever make a pie.

I'll rethink my prejudices and give lard a try again.

Kathy Foster, Rutherfordton, North Carolina

APPLESAUCE BROWNIES

The proof is not in the pudding, but in the applesauce, which makes these brownies extra moist and sweet. Applesauce often is added to baked goods to add moisture without fat. No one can pass up these gooey morsels with frosting on top.   Makes 2 dozen

½ cup lard, softened, plus
more for greasing the pan

1 cup all-purpose unbleached flour,
plus more for dusting the pan

1 cup granulated sugar

2 eggs

½ cup plus 1 tablespoon applesauce

1 teaspoon vanilla extract

3 tablespoons unsweetened cocoa

½ teaspoon baking powder

¼ teaspoon baking soda

¼ teaspoon salt

½ cup chopped walnuts

1 tablespoon salted butter

1 cup confectioners' sugar

Preheat the oven to 350°F. Grease a 9 by 9-inch baking pan with lard; lightly dust with flour and set aside.

In a large bowl, using an electric mixer on low speed, cream together the lard and granulated sugar. Add the eggs and continue beating. Add ½ cup of applesauce and the vanilla; beat until smooth.

In a large bowl, sift together the flour, 2 tablespoons of cocoa, the baking powder, baking soda, and salt; add gradually to the creamed mixture and mix well. Fold in the walnuts.

Spread the batter in the prepared pan. Bake for 35 minutes. While still warm, cut into squares or bars; remove from the pan and cool on a wire rack.

To make the frosting, combine the butter, the remaining 1 tablespoon of applesauce, the remaining 1 tablespoon of cocoa, and the confectioners' sugar in a medium bowl; blend until smooth. If you prefer a thicker frosting, add a little more applesauce and confectioners' sugar. Spread the frosting on the cooled brownies.

STRAINING THE LARD

Lard comes from big pigs! They make noise and are bigger than the men who raise them. In the 1940s, all pigs were bigger and fatter. The biggest on our place was the grouchy old sow that could no longer raise the desired number of piglets. After a single, swift plunge of Grandpa Miller's very sharp knife, the sow was soon hoisted into the scalding vat in preparation to being scraped clean.

As a girl, I didn't pay attention to how many family and friends gathered to butcher or even if they usually did more than one pig at a time. Considering the large vat, they probably butchered for more than one family at a time. Nor do I remember how they set up tables to do the cutting. I do remember Grandma rendering/cooking the fat in her big black soup kettle in the yard.

By afternoon, she began my favorite part of the process—straining the lard. The liquid in the pot was dipped into a bucket and strained through a white cloth. What remained of the cooked fat was put into the press, and the last drips squeezed out to save for cooking and other tasks. I really liked to see it come out brown and almost crisp. After squeezing, it made tastier "cracklings." The pork rinds in the store now don't really compare in taste or texture.

My other grandma couldn't give me her recipe for her delicious oatmeal cookies, so I asked her to make them while I measured her pinches, spoonfuls, and cupfuls of spices, flour, oatmeal, and other ingredients. Then came her admonition that they would never taste right made with melted Crisco—they should be made with lard. And she was right.

Verna Rundell, Syracuse, Kansas

CHOCOLATE SYRUP BROWNIES
with CREAMY CHOCOLATE ICING

When nothing but chocolate will do, turn to these intensely flavored dark brownies with icing. To make your own chocolate syrup, combine 1 cup of unsweetened cocoa, 1½ cups of sugar, a pinch of salt, 1½ cups of water, and 1 teaspoon of vanilla extract in a saucepan over medium-high heat. Heat to boiling, stirring constantly, for 3 to 5 minutes, until the syrup thickens. Cool and store in a jar in the refrigerator. It's more work than buying a squeeze bottle or a can, but your effort will be rewarded with the rich chocolate taste. Makes 2 dozen

½ cup lard, softened, plus more for greasing the pan

1 cup chocolate syrup

¾ cup sifted cake flour

¼ teaspoon baking powder

¼ teaspoon salt

2 eggs, well beaten

¾ cup chopped pecans

1 teaspoon vanilla extract

ICING

1 tablespoon salted butter

1 tablespoon lard

3 tablespoons milk

2 tablespoons cocoa

1 teaspoon vanilla extract

1 to 1½ cups confectioners' sugar

Preheat the oven to 350°F. Grease a 9 by 9-inch pan with lard and set aside.

In a large bowl, using the back of a spoon, cream the lard until fluffy and creamy. Add the chocolate syrup gradually, continuing to work with the spoon, until light.

In a separate bowl, sift together the sifted flour, baking powder, and salt; add a quarter of the flour mixture to the lard mixture while beating with the spoon. Add the eggs, then the remaining sifted ingredients, the pecans, and vanilla. Spread the batter in the prepared pan.

Bake for 35 minutes, until a toothpick inserted in the center comes out clean. Set on a wire rack to cool slightly.

To make the icing, melt the butter and lard in a small saucepan over low heat. Whisk in the milk, cocoa, vanilla, and enough confectioners' sugar to bring the icing to a spreading consistency. Remove the pan from the heat and cool slightly. Spread the icing over the warm brownies, then immediately cut them into squares.

SPICY PUMPKIN BARS
with CREAM CHEESE ICING

The day after Thanksgiving is a great time to make these bars using leftover fresh pureed pumpkin. If you haven't got any, though, use good old Libby's in a can (pure pumpkin, not pumpkin pie mix), which won top honors in a taste test for its creamy texture and mild sweetness. You can substitute pureed butternut squash in this recipe for an equally sweet taste and pleasing texture.   Makes 16

BARS

½ cup lard, softened, plus
more for greasing the pan

2 cups all-purpose unbleached flour

4 teaspoons baking powder

1¼ teaspoons cinnamon

1 teaspoon nutmeg

1 teaspoon ginger

½ teaspoon salt

1 cup brown sugar, packed

¼ cup granulated sugar

4 eggs

1 (15-ounce) can pureed pumpkin

ICING

1 (3-ounce) package cream
cheese, softened

1 tablespoon butter, softened

1 tablespoon milk

1 teaspoon vanilla extract

2½ cups confectioners' sugar

Preheat the oven to 350°F. Grease a 15½ by 10½-inch jelly roll pan with lard; set aside.

In a medium bowl, sift together the flour, baking powder, cinnamon, nutmeg, ginger, and salt; set aside. In a large bowl, cream together the lard and sugars using an electric mixer on medium speed until light and fluffy. Add the eggs, one at a time, beating well after each addition. Beat in the pumpkin. Stir in the dry ingredients gradually, mixing well. Spread the mixture in the prepared pan.

Bake for 30 minutes, until a toothpick inserted in the center comes out clean. Cool in the pan on a wire rack.

To make the icing, combine the cream cheese, butter, milk, and vanilla in a medium bowl; add half the confectioners' sugar and beat until smooth. Add the remaining confectioners' sugar and beat until no lumps remain. Using an offset spatula, spread the icing over the cooled bars and cut into pieces.

PEANUT BUTTER BROWNIES

If you love a good blondie—a brownie with a brown sugar rather than a cocoa base—and the flavor of peanut butter, then you'll adore these brownies. This recipe is a big batch—it makes 80 brownies in three large pans, so save this for your kid's bake sale or your next family reunion, or reduce it by a third for a more typical yield of 2 dozen. Makes 80

½ cup lard, softened, plus more for greasing the pan

6 eggs

3 cups granulated sugar

1½ cups brown sugar, packed

1 cup peanut butter

1 tablespoon vanilla extract

4 cups all-purpose unbleached flour

1½ tablespoons baking powder

1½ teaspoons salt

1 cup chopped peanuts

Preheat the oven to 350°F. Grease two 15½ by 10½ by 1-inch pans or three 13 by 9 by 2-inch pans with lard; set aside.

In a very large bowl, combine the eggs, sugars, peanut butter, lard, and vanilla; using an electric mixer on medium speed, beat well. Add the flour, baking powder, and salt; mix until smooth.

Distribute the batter evenly into the prepared pans and sprinkle each pan with the nuts.

Bake for 20 minutes, until golden brown and a toothpick inserted in the center comes out clean. Cool completely on wire racks. Cut into bars.

OATMEAL BARS

If your family loves oatmeal cookies, kick 'em up a notch with these snack bars bursting with chocolate, butterscotch, and oatmeal. There's no shortage of oatmeal in these bars—3 cups—which means they deliver the nutty, oaty flavor and chewy texture you'd expect. Makes 12 to 20 (depending on whether they're chewy or crispy)

¾ cup lard, softened, plus more for greasing the pans

1 cup brown sugar, packed

½ cup granulated sugar

1 extra large egg or 2 small eggs

¼ cup water

1 teaspoon vanilla extract

½ teaspoon rum extract

1 cup all-purpose unbleached flour

1 teaspoon salt

½ teaspoon baking soda

3 cups old-fashioned oats

½ cup chocolate chips

½ cup butterscotch chips

Preheat the oven to 350°F. For thin, crispy bars, grease one 9 by 12-inch pan and one 8 by 8-inch pan with lard; for chewy bars, grease one 13 by 9-inch baking pan. Set aside.

In a large bowl, combine the lard, sugars, egg, water, and vanilla and rum extracts. Using an electric mixer on low speed, beat until fluffy. Add the flour, salt, and baking soda and mix well. Stir in the oats and chips.

Press the dough into the prepared pan(s) and bake for 20 minutes, until lightly browned. Cool completely in the pans on wire racks and then cut into bars.

Chapter 5

PIES

PERFECT PASTRY

This recipe is for savory pastry shells designed to be prebaked, then filled with eggs for quiche, custard, or pumpkin, and finished cooking as the specific recipe instructs. Whenever you see "use your favorite pie crust recipe," turn to this recipe. Bake the pastry flat (rather than in a pie dish), with the edges folded up slightly, and use it for the base of a rustic tart.   **Makes 3 9-inch pie shells**

1 teaspoon salt

2 cups all-purpose unbleached flour, sifted

¾ cup lard, cold and coarsely chopped

¼ cup cold milk

Preheat the oven to 450°F.

In a large bowl, mix the salt and flour; using a pastry blender, cut in the lard to make a coarse, crumbly mixture. Blend in the milk gradually, gently tossing with a fork, until the dough sticks together in a ball.

Turn the dough onto a lightly floured surface and divide it into 3 equal parts. Place in pie pans or flat on baking sheets; using a fork, prick the unbaked shells thoroughly before baking.

Bake for 15 to 20 minutes, until golden brown. Set on a wire rack to cool before filling. Finish baking as directed by your recipe.

FROZEN PIE CRUST

If your holidays are spent rushing from one task to the next, and the little things—such as homemade pie crusts—often get set aside due to lack of time, this year spend a day in early November making this recipe. You'll end up with not just the shells you need for the holidays but for the whole new year!   Makes 21 single 9-inch pie shells

1 (5-pound) bag all-purpose unbleached flour

2 tablespoons salt

3 pounds lard, cold and coarsely chopped

1 cup light corn syrup

3 cups cold water

In a very large bowl, mix together the flour and salt. Using an electric mixer on medium-low speed, cut in the lard until the mixture resembles coarse crumbs. Stir in the corn syrup and water and mix until the dough sticks together. Divide the dough into fist-sized balls and place in individual quart-sized freezer bags. Place the individual bags in a large, resealable freezer bag (2-gallon size) and put in the freezer.

To use: Remove 1 ball of dough for each crust needed. Let thaw for about 1 hour at room temperature, or defrost in the refrigerator overnight. Roll out the crust as needed. The dough will be soft, and you can refreeze any unused dough.

PIE CRUST

Here's a basic recipe for pie dough, plus a crash course in Making Pie Crust 101. Try your hand at making a charming lattice-topped pie, but get your camera ready. The finished pie will be so beautiful you'll want to snap a photo for your scrapbook. **Makes 4 single or 2 9-inch double crusts**

3 cups all-purpose unbleached flour

1 teaspoon salt

1¼ cups lard, cold and coarsely chopped

1 egg

5½ tablespoons water

1 teaspoon vinegar

In a large bowl, combine the flour and salt. Using a pastry blender, cut in the lard until the mixture is very fine. In a separate bowl, beat together the egg, water, and vinegar. Make a small well in the flour mixture and add the liquid; mix just until the dough comes together in a ball. Divide the dough into 4 equal pieces and flatten into disks; wrap individually in plastic and refrigerate for at least 30 minutes before rolling.

To make a double-crust pie with a solid top crust, roll out 2 disks of dough about 1 inch larger than the pie plate. Fit one crust into the bottom of the pie plate. Fill the pie with the desired filling; slightly moisten the edge of the bottom crust. Take the second crust, fold it in half, gently place it over the pie filling, and unfold, centering it on the pie plate; press the edges into the bottom crust to seal. Trim the excess dough to leave an overhang of about ¾ inch. Crimp or flute the edges with your fingers. To allow steam to escape, gently prick the top crust with a fork several times or slash vents with a sharp knife.

For a lattice-top crust, roll the second crust to a diameter of about 13 inches (for a 9-inch pie) and cut the dough into eighteen ½-inch-wide strips. Fill the pie and slightly moisten the edge of the bottom crust. Place 9 strips evenly across the filling, leaving space between and allowing the excess to hang over the edge of the bottom crust. Trim the excess dough and press the ends of the strips into the edge of the bottom crust to seal. Place the other 9 strips across the first set in a crisscross pattern; trim and press the second set of strips to seal. Fold up the bottom crust to cover the ends of the lattice strips, then crimp or flute with your fingers.

To make a glazed top crust, beat 1 egg white and brush on the unbaked top crust; sprinkle with sugar.

For a brown crust, brush the unbaked top crust with milk or cream, then sprinkle with sugar.

Bake the pies according to the recipe.

BUTCHERING HOGS AND MAKING LARD

When I was a child, we butchered hogs every winter. The men did it outside on a cold day. Neighbors sometimes got together to do the scalding, scraping, and all the duties of butchering. The entrails were dumped into an old tub to haul off later. We youngsters were ghoulishly entertained by seeing what came out of the insides of a hog.

One of my highlighted memories of childhood was the day we worked up the meat. Our entire family of five gathered in the kitchen. We cut the fat in small pieces to put in a big pan on the wood cookstove to render the lard. It was cooked slowly and stirred often to keep it from scorching, then it was strained through a clean white cloth and baking soda was added to keep it nice and white. My brother would turn the handle on the meat grinder to make sausage. Daddy trimmed the hams and shoulders for curing and prepared the other cuts of pork. For supper, we always had tenderloin, brown gravy, and hot biscuits made with lard.

Every Sunday morning, we made pies for Sunday dinner. We used lard to make the rich, flaky crust. In the cast-iron skillet, we fried chicken in pure lard. What fresh, delicious Sunday dinners we had!

I used to take pies to the bank where I worked, and several people complimented me on my crust. When I told those city boys the crusts were made with pig lard, they just rolled their eyes—and kept right on eating.

I am a grandmother now and still use lard to make pie crusts. I don't usually measure when I make them, but I will attempt to send my recipe. And one doesn't need a recipe for frying chicken in lard—just fry it.

Joyce Surface, West Plains, Missouri

JOYCE'S PIE CRUST Makes 1 9-inch crust

**1¼ cups all-purpose white flour,
plus more for dusting**

1 teaspoon salt

½ cup lard

3 tablespoons cold water

Mix together the flour and salt. Cut in the lard until small crumbles form. Add the cold water and mix until all the crumbs are stuck together. Flour the working surface and roll out the crusts to fit in a pie plate for a single crust, then follow the directions for whatever pie you want to make.

Double the recipe for fruit pies and bake according to your fruit pie recipe.

REFUGEE PIE CRUST

Refugees in camps all over the world receive meager rations consisting of wheat or oats, sugar or molasses, salt, and oil or lard with which to prepare their meals. Take note of the small proportions and unusual substitutions for the usual pie crust ingredients. This recipe makes a small crust—the total volume is just over 1 cup—so it's best rolled thinly and pressed into a small pan. Surely, it would make an impromptu dessert for one. **Makes 1 6-inch crust**

¼ cup lard, softened, plus more for greasing the pan

1 tablespoon sugar

¼ cup all-purpose unbleached flour

¼ teaspoon salt

1 tablespoon molasses or dark corn syrup

¼ cup quick-cooking rolled oats

Fresh fruit and whipped cream, for serving

Preheat the oven to 350°F. Grease a small pie pan with lard and set aside.

In a medium bowl, cream together the lard and sugar with a spoon. Add the flour, salt, and molasses. Stir in the oats and mix well. Pack into the bottom of the prepared pan.

Bake for 15 minutes, until golden. Remove from the oven. Fill with fresh fruit and top with whipped cream.

CHERRY CUSTARD PIE

This ridiculously simple cherry pie is just the recipe you'll be seeking come the dog days of summer when the heat is sapping your motivation to cook. You'll have a cherry pie in under an hour, including making the crust and baking. Use the single pie crust recipe given, or pull one of the frozen pie crust balls (page 145) out of the freezer. **Serves 8**

CRUST

1 cup all-purpose unbleached flour

½ cup lard, cold and coarsely chopped

¼ cup ice water

FILLING

1 cup fresh or canned cherries, pitted

½ cup sugar

2 eggs, beaten

1 cup milk

Preheat the oven to 350°F.

Place the flour in a large bowl. Using a pastry blender, cut in the lard until the mixture resembles pea-sized crumbs. Add the ice water, 1 tablespoon at a time, mixing until a ball forms. Turn the dough onto a floured surface and roll out to 2 inches larger than your pie pan. Line the pie plate with the pastry and fold under the excess dough. Crimp or flute the edge with your fingers.

In a medium bowl, combine the cherries, sugar, eggs, and milk and mix well. Pour into the pastry crust.

Bake for 45 minutes, until the filling is set and the crust is golden brown. Cool completely before slicing.

BUMBLEBERRY PIE

Bumbleberry pie is just like it sounds—a jumble of fruit, usually mixed berries, baked into a pie. Also known as "kitchen sink pie," the bumbleberry pie's origins lie in the pioneer cooks of America and their propensity for using whatever was at hand rather than following a set recipe—to prepare meals for big, hungry families. This recipe is for two double-crusted pies; feel free to use any fruit you've got in the same proportions. **Makes 2 9-inch pies**

5½ cups plus ⅔ cup all-purpose unbleached flour

¼ teaspoon salt

2 cups lard, cold and coarsely chopped

1 egg plus 1 egg yolk

1 tablespoon vinegar

¾ cup ice water

2 cups fresh or frozen chopped rhubarb

2 cups fresh or frozen blueberries

2 cups fresh or frozen raspberries

2 cups fresh or frozen sliced strawberries

4 cups chopped peeled baking apples

2 cups sugar

2 tablespoons lemon juice

Ice cream or sweetened whipped cream, for serving

In a very large bowl, combine 5½ cups of flour with the salt; using a pastry blender, cut in the lard until crumbly. In a separate bowl, whisk together the whole egg, the vinegar, and half of the ice water; sprinkle over the dry ingredients and toss with a fork. If needed, add more water, 1 tablespoon at a time, until the dough can be formed into a ball (discard the remaining ice water). Divide the dough into 4 balls and press into disks. Wrap each disk in plastic and chill for at least 30 minutes.

Preheat the oven to 350°F. Remove the dough from the refrigerator and unwrap.

Place the dough on a lightly floured surface; roll out 2 disks to fit two 9-inch pie pans. Press one crust into each pan, leaving a 1-inch overhang.

In a large bowl, combine the rhubarb, berries, apples, sugar, the remaining ⅔ cup of flour, and the lemon juice; mix well. Distribute the filling evenly between the 2 pies.

Roll out the remaining 2 dough disks for the top crusts; moisten the overhanging bottom crust with water. Place the top crust over the pie and trim the edges. Seal and flute the edges.

In a small bowl, combine the remaining egg yolk with a little water (1 to 2 tablespoons) and beat well; brush over the top crusts. Using a sharp knife, cut vents in the top crust.

Bake for 50 to 60 minutes, until the juices are bubbling and the crust is golden brown. Cool completely before slicing. Serve with ice cream or sweetened whipped cream.

LARD SAVED LITTLE BROTHER

When reading about lard, I was reminded of a time when two of my brothers put another brother into a milk can and rolled him down a hill. When they tried to retrieve him, they found he was stuck. They could not get him out of the can.

Mom solved the problem by having him lower himself further into the can, then she proceeded to grease the inside with lard. After thoroughly greasing the can, she was able to extract my brother.

Mom always said she couldn't make good pie crust without lard, so she made sure she always had some on hand until her death in 2009. Thank you for bringing this pleasant memory back to me.

Billie Bonecutter, Jefferson City, Missouri

FRIED FRUIT PIES

If you loved Hostess Fruit Pies or those fast-food hot apple turnovers when you were young, this more sophisticated version will take you way back, and you'll be surprised at how much better they taste. Use your favorite dried fruit—apricots, apples, cherries, blueberries, peaches—or even lemon curd for the filling. Makes 8

FILLING

12 ounces dried fruit of your choice, cut into small pieces

2 to 3 tablespoons sugar

¾ teaspoon cinnamon

½ teaspoon nutmeg

CRUST

2 cups all-purpose unbleached flour

1 teaspoon baking powder

½ teaspoon salt

¼ cup lard, cold and coarsely chopped, plus more for frying

½ cup milk

1 egg, slightly beaten

In a medium saucepan, place the fruit and enough water to cover it. Heat over medium-high heat until boiling. Reduce the heat, cover, and simmer until tender, 20 to 25 minutes. Drain. Transfer the fruit to a bowl and stir in the sugar, cinnamon, and nutmeg; set aside.

In a large bowl, whisk together the flour, baking powder, and salt. Using a pastry blender, cut in the lard until the mixture resembles coarse crumbs. In a separate large bowl, mix together the milk and egg. Stir the flour mixture into the milk mixture until all the flour is moistened and the dough sticks together.

Gather the dough into a ball and cut in half. Using a rolling pin, roll out each dough half on a lightly floured board to a ⅛-inch thickness. Using a 6-inch bowl as a guide, cut each half into four 6-inch rounds. Place ¼ cup of the fruit mixture in the center of each pastry round. Moisten the edge of the pastry and fold over; press the edges firmly with a fork to seal.

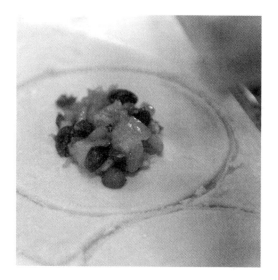

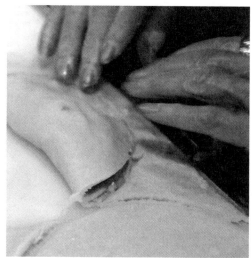

In a deep cast-iron skillet, heat the lard to 375°F and 3 inches deep. In batches, place the pies in the hot fat and fry for 1½ to 2 minutes on each side, until golden brown. Drain on paper towels. Serve warm.

PEACHEESY PIE

In October 1964, Janis Risley of Melbourne, Florida, won the Pillsbury Bake-Off with this combination. Her original recipe calls for a box of refrigerated Pillsbury pie crust, of course, but ours suggests a homemade crust, made with lard. The award-winning peach pie is flavored with pumpkin pie spices, and has a cheesecake layer sandwiched between the filling and top crust. It would be hard to beat this peach pie—as a matter of fact, nothing did! Serves 8

CRUST

2 cups all-purpose unbleached flour

1 teaspoon salt

⅔ cup lard, cold and coarsely chopped

6 to 7 tablespoons peach syrup

FILLING

1 (28-ounce) can sliced cling peaches, drained, syrup reserved

½ cup sugar

2 tablespoons cornstarch

2 tablespoons corn syrup

2 teaspoons pumpkin pie spice

2 teaspoons vanilla extract

2 tablespoons salted butter

CHEESECAKE LAYER

2 eggs, lightly beaten

⅓ cup sugar

1 tablespoon lemon juice

2 tablespoons peach syrup

1 (3-ounce) package cream cheese, softened

½ cup sour cream

To make the crust, combine the flour and salt in a large bowl. Using a pastry blender, cut in the lard until the mixture resembles coarse crumbs. Sprinkle the peach syrup over the mixture while stirring with a fork until the dough sticks together in a ball. Divide the dough in half.

On a floured surface, roll out half the dough to a circle 1½ inches larger than an inverted 9-inch pie pan. Fit the crust into the pan; flute the edge using your fingers. Set aside.

Preheat the oven to 425°F.

To prepare the filling, combine the peach slices, sugar, cornstarch, corn syrup, pumpkin pie spice, and vanilla in a large bowl; set aside.

To prepare the cheesecake layer, in a small saucepan over medium heat, combine the eggs, sugar, lemon juice, and peach syrup. Heat to boiling, stirring constantly, until thick. Remove from the heat.

In a large bowl, combine the cream cheese and sour cream. Pour in the hot peach syrup mixture and beat with an electric mixer on medium speed until smooth.

Fill the prepared pie crust with the uncooked peach filling. Dot with the butter. Pour the cheesecake mixture over the top.

On a floured surface, roll out the remaining dough. Using a 2½-inch cookie or biscuit cutter, cut into circles; brush the circles with the remaining peach syrup. Arrange the dough circles on top of the pie.

Bake for 10 minutes; reduce the oven temperature to 350°F, cover the edge with foil or an aluminum pie ring, then bake for 30 to 35 minutes more, until the crust is deep golden brown. Cool completely before slicing.

APPLE—MAPLE—RAISIN PIE

This apple pie is so much more—with a creamy, spicy filling infused with cinnamon, maple syrup, and cardamom. Every person in the house will be drawn to the kitchen as the aroma wafts through the air. For the truest maple flavor, use only pure maple syrup. Serve with cinnamon ice cream, hard sauce (page 198), or heavy cream. **Serves 8**

2⅔ cups plus ¼ cup all-purpose unbleached flour, plus more for dusting

1½ teaspoons salt

1 cup lard, cold and coarsely chopped

7 to 8 tablespoons cold water

9 cups apples (about 2½ pounds), peeled, cored, and quartered

½ cup raisins

¾ cup pure maple syrup

¼ cup heavy whipping cream

1½ teaspoons cinnamon

½ teaspoon ground cardamom

1 tablespoon milk

Preheat the oven to 375°F.

In a large bowl, combine 2⅔ cups flour and 1 teaspoon salt. Using a pastry blender, cut in the lard until the mixture forms pea-sized chunks. Sprinkle with cold water, 1 tablespoon at a time, and toss lightly with a fork until the dough sticks together in a ball. Divide the dough into two equal parts. Press to form two 5- to 6-inch disks. Dust each disk lightly with flour on both sides.

On a dampened countertop, place one disk on a sheet of wax paper; cover with another sheet. Roll the dough to a ⅛-inch thickness. Peel off the top sheet of wax paper. Invert a 10-inch pie plate on the crust and trim to 1 inch larger than the dish. Turn the pastry into the pie plate and remove the other sheet of wax paper. Using a knife, trim the edge even with the pie plate. Moisten the edge of the pastry with water.

To make the filling, toss the apples and raisins with the maple syrup, the remaining ¼ cup flour, the remaining ½ teaspoon salt, the cream, cinnamon, and cardamom. Mound the filling in the pie shell.

Roll the top crust in the same manner as the bottom. Flip the dough onto the filled pie and trim ½ inch beyond the edge of the pie plate. Fold the top edge under the bottom crust. Press together and flute using your fingers. Brush the crust with the milk. Using a sharp knife, cut vents in the top crust.

Bake for 1¼ to 1½ hours, until the crust is golden brown and the filling is bubbling. Cover the pie loosely with foil to prevent overbrowning, if necessary. Do not overbake. Cool on a wire rack for at least 1 hour before serving.

GREAT CHRISTMAS PIES

I was born in 1945, and I still remember my mother cooking with lard. I also remember my father going out to a farm on Christmas to get real whipping cream.

My grandchildren raised "grease pigs" this summer. When we had them butchered, we asked for the lard. I made pies for Christmas and was very pleased with the way the pie dough handled.

Nadine Taylor, Northwood, Ohio

CHERRY PIE

A favorite of cowboys on cattle drives, this classic cherry pie was often cooked in a cast-iron skillet over a campfire. The "cookie" (chuck wagon cook) substituted honey for sugar when the chuck box ran out, and the recipe has remained that way since. Gather 'round the 'hands and serve this pie with heaping scoops of vanilla ice cream. Watch them dig in with gusto. **Serves 8**

Pastry for double-crust pie

Egg white, melted butter, or flour (optional)

4 tablespoons cornstarch

¼ cup cherry juice

1¼ cups honey

3 cups red sour cherries, pitted

1 tablespoon butter

Make the Pie Crust (page 146) recipe. On a floured surface, roll one portion of dough to about 3 inches larger than your pie plate. Fold the dough in half and gently unfold into the pie plate. Press the dough gently to fit the pie plate. Using a knife, trim the edges, leaving a ¾-inch overhang. Do not prick the bottom crust! To prevent a soggy crust, brush it with an egg white or melted butter, or sprinkle lightly with flour, if using.

Roll the second portion of dough to a diameter of about 13 inches and cut the dough into eighteen ½-inch-wide strips. Leave the strips on the cutting board until you're ready for the top crust.

Preheat the oven to 425°F.

To make the filling, combine the cornstarch and cherry juice in a saucepan over low heat; add the honey and cook until the mixture is thick, stirring frequently. Remove from the heat, and add the cherries and butter, stirring well. Set aside to cool.

Pour the filling into the pastry-lined pie plate.

To make a lattice-top crust, follow the instructions on page 147.

Bake for 10 minutes. Reduce the heat to 350°F and bake for an additional 20 minutes, until the filling is bubbling and the crust is golden brown. Cover loosely with foil to prevent overbrowning, if necessary. Cool on a wire rack.

CLARA'S TIPS ON PIE DOUGH

Lard is making a comeback? Great news! Among my favorite memories is learning to make pies with my grandmother Clara in Southampton, New York. I spent hours at her side learning her technique for making pie crust, and one of her essential ingredients was lard—no substitutes. You had to work just the right amount into the flour mixture, then make a small well in the middle for the ice water. With her thumb in the well, she would spin the bowl, flinging water lightly into the crust, mentioning every single time that the trick to a flaky crust was to make sure the water was ice cold, to use as little as possible, and to handle the dough very little, just enough to form a ball. Her crusts were always perfect, mine not so much. I can still see her beautiful old fingers, bent from arthritis, gently working the water into the dough.

The recipe? That's a tough one. After adding salt, baking soda, and baking powder in pinches to an estimate of flour, she would cut off a sliver of lard without measuring. When I make pies today, I just imagine she's standing there looking over my shoulder and somehow it works out, though mine are never quite like hers. The tough part has been finding the lard! It's been getting harder over the years' as many grocery stores not only don't stock it but most clerks have never heard of it. I've taken to asking the butcher. It's wonderful that your cookbook may help to bring it back to its rightful place.

And for you lard and music lovers out there, nothing beats the great children's song "Lard," by the Green Chili Jam Band. Check it out on iTunes.

Susan Reres, Afton, Virginia

MOLASSES CRUMB PIE

This Pennsylvania Dutch and Amish specialty is more commonly known as "shoofly pie." It's believed that shoofly pie may be so called because the sweet ingredients—molasses and brown sugar—beckoned flies, which needed to be "shooed" away. Serve warm with sweetened whipped cream. Serves 8

½ **cup mild molasses**

1 **egg yolk**

½ **teaspoon baking soda**

¾ **cup boiling water**

2¼ **cups all-purpose unbleached flour**

½ **cup brown sugar, packed**

¾ **teaspoon salt**

½ **teaspoon cinnamon**

⅛ **teaspoon nutmeg**

⅛ **teaspoon ginger**

⅛ **teaspoon cloves**

6 to 8 **tablespoons lard, softened**

4 to 6 **tablespoons cold water**

In a large bowl, combine the molasses, egg yolk, and baking soda. Pour in the boiling water and blend; set aside.

In a separate bowl, combine ¾ cup of flour, the brown sugar, ¼ teaspoon of salt, the cinnamon, nutmeg, ginger, and cloves; using a pastry blender, cut in 2 tablespoons lard. Set aside.

Sift the remaining 1½ cups of flour with the remaining ½ teaspoon of salt; cut in the remaining 4 to 6 tablespoons of lard. Add only enough cold water to hold the dough together. Turn the dough onto a lightly floured surface and roll to fit your pie plate.

Preheat the oven to 450°F.

Line the pie plate with the pastry, pressing gently to fit. Alternately, layer in the spice mixture and the molasses mixture, ending with the spice mixture.

Bake until the crust edges start to brown. Reduce the oven temperature to 375°F and continue baking until firm, about 20 minutes. Cool on a wire rack.

GREEN TOMATO PIE

This late-season southern classic is traditional fare that originated during the Depression. Depression-era folks never let a thing go to waste, so with necessity being the mother of invention, this green tomato pie was created by a farm wife who wanted to put an apple pie on the table but had no apples. Something strange but delicious happens to green tomatoes when they are prepared in this pie. Serve this sweet—not savory—pie with ice cream, heavy cream, or hard sauce (page 198). **Serves 8**

CRUST

2¼ cups all-purpose unbleached flour

½ teaspoon salt

⅔ cup lard, cold and coarsely chopped

⅓ cup cold water

FILLING

3 cups unpeeled thinly sliced green tomatoes

½ cup brown sugar, packed

2 tablespoons flour

1 teaspoon cinnamon

¼ teaspoon nutmeg

½ cup mild molasses

½ cup water

To make the crust, combine the flour and salt in a large bowl. Using a pastry blender or two knives, cut in the lard until the mixture resembles peas. Do not overmix. Add the cold water gradually, sprinkling 1 tablespoon at a time over the mixture. Toss lightly with a fork until all the flour has been moistened and the pastry sticks together in a ball—it should not feel wet.

Divide the dough into 2 equal portions. Roll the dough into 2 round balls, handling as little as possible. On a lightly floured board, roll one dough ball to a ⅛-inch thickness and 1 inch larger than the diameter of the edge of the pie plate. Gently place the bottom crust in the pie plate. Place in the refrigerator.

Preheat the oven to 425°F.

Place the tomatoes in a large saucepan and cover with boiling water; let stand for 10 minutes, then drain and dry. Pile the tomato slices in the unbaked pastry shell.

In a bowl, combine the brown sugar, flour, and spices. Add the molasses and water. Pour the mixture over the tomatoes.

Roll out the remaining dough for the top crust. After filling the bottom crust, place the top crust carefully over the filling. Moisten the edge of the top crust with cold water. Press together the edges of the top and bottom crusts tightly using a fork, or flute with your fingers.

Bake for 15 minutes. Reduce the oven temperature to 375°F and continue baking for an additional 30 minutes. Cool for 15 minutes before slicing.

BEST PIE CRUST AROUND

We grew up in the country near the homes of both sets of grandparents, and my "double" cousins. (A brother and sister married sister and brother.) I remember going to one grandparents' house where there was always a consistent stream of homemade molasses cookies—made with lard, of course—waiting for us. My mother would tell how the huge cast-iron kettle, now used for decoration in a flower bed, once had been used to render the lard and suet in the fall.

My mother's baked beans were well known in the neighborhood as the best, and she credited the taste to her use of fresh side pork. We were always confused at how we got to eat the beans as a Friday night meat substitute, however.

The one thing my mother was most proud of, though, was her pie crust. I remember how she insisted I learn how to make it, because, in her mind, mastering perfect pie crust was like a degree from Le Cordon Bleu. Recently, when offered some fat from a locally butchered pig, I jumped at the chance to take it, and now we'll see if I have inherited Mom's knack of creating the best pie crust around.

Jan Look, Hastings, Michigan

Chapter 6

CAKES

JAM CUPCAKES

Peanut butter and jelly sandwiches . . . a child's favorite lunch-box meal that may or may not be outgrown. If you're a kid at heart—or have kids who love PB&Js—whip up these jam cupcakes with peanut butter frosting.   **Makes 1½ dozen**

½ cup lard, softened, plus more
for greasing the pans

2 cups sifted cake flour

½ teaspoon salt

½ teaspoon cinnamon

1 teaspoon nutmeg

1 teaspoon baking soda

1 cup granulated sugar

2 eggs, beaten

½ cup buttermilk

1 cup strawberry or raspberry jam

FROSTING

1 cup creamy peanut butter

5 tablespoons salted butter, softened

½ teaspoon vanilla extract

Pinch of salt

1 cup confectioners' sugar

⅓ cup heavy cream

Crushed peanuts (optional)

Preheat the oven to 375°F. Grease two standard muffin tins with lard and set aside.

In a medium bowl, sift together the sifted flour, salt, cinnamon, nutmeg, and baking soda; set aside.

In a large bowl, using an electric mixer on medium-low speed, cream the granulated sugar with the lard until fluffy. Add the eggs and beat. Alternately add the flour mixture and the buttermilk to the creamed mixture, beating well after each addition. Fold in the jam.

Pour the batter into the prepared muffin tins, filling two-thirds full.

Bake for 20 to 25 minutes, until a toothpick inserted in the center of a cupcake comes out clean. Cool on wire racks for 5 minutes, then turn out to cool completely.

To make the frosting, combine the peanut butter, butter, vanilla, and salt in a large bowl. Using an electric mixer on medium-low speed, beat until creamy. Slowly add the confectioners' sugar and cream and beat on high speed for 1 to 2 minutes, until the frosting is smooth. Spread the frosting on the cupcakes and top with the crushed peanuts, if using.

PINEAPPLE—COCONUT CUPCAKES

Coconut and pineapple are such a classic tropical combination. The sweet, intense pineapple flavor of these cupcakes marries well with the nuttiness of coconut—they won't disappoint even the biggest sweet tooth. Use cake flour for the most tender, delicate texture. If you don't have cake flour on hand, make your own using this formula: 2 tablespoons cornstarch + ⅞ cup all-purpose unbleached flour = 1 cup cake flour. Makes 2 dozen

½ cup lard, softened

1 cup granulated sugar

2 eggs, beaten

1 teaspoon vanilla extract

2½ cups sifted cake flour

3 teaspoons baking powder

½ teaspoon salt

¼ cup water

½ cup pineapple juice

⅔ cup crushed pineapple, drained

1 cup finely shredded sweetened coconut

GLAZE

2 cups confectioners' sugar

2 to 3 tablespoons pineapple juice

Toasted coconut, for topping

Preheat the oven to 350°F. Line two muffin tins with paper liners and set aside.

In a large bowl, cream together the lard and granulated sugar using an electric mixer on low speed. Add the eggs and vanilla, mixing well. Sift together the sifted flour, baking powder, and salt. In a small bowl, combine the water and pineapple juice.

Alternately add the flour mixture and the pineapple juice and water to the creamed mixture, beating well after each addition. Fold in the pineapple and coconut.

Spoon the batter into the muffin cups, filling half full. Bake for 25 minutes, until a toothpick inserted in the center comes out clean. Cool completely on a wire rack.

To make the glaze, whip together the confectioners' sugar and pineapple juice in a small bowl until smooth. Add more pineapple juice as needed to get a thin glaze. Dip the top of each cupcake in the glaze, just coating lightly. Then top with the toasted coconut and serve.

ROOT BEER CUPCAKES

Root beer candy, root beer pop, and whipped topping come together for this root beer float in a cupcake! There's no end to the possibilities of this good-times dessert. Substitute with your favorite pop—cola, lemon-lime, orange—and pick a complementary hard candy. These cupcakes are spot on for kids' birthday parties. Makes 1½ dozen

2 cups all-purpose unbleached flour

1 cup brown sugar, packed

⅔ cup finely crushed
root beer–flavored hard candy

1 teaspoon baking powder

½ teaspoon baking soda

½ teaspoon salt

⅛ teaspoon allspice

⅛ teaspoon cinnamon

1 cup root beer

½ cup lard, melted and cooled slightly

2 eggs

2 cups frozen whipped topping, thawed

Preheat the oven to 350°F. Line two standard muffin tins with paper liners and set aside.

In a large bowl, combine the flour, brown sugar, ⅓ cup candy, the baking powder, baking soda, salt, allspice, cinnamon, root beer, lard, and eggs. Using an electric mixer on low speed, blend until moistened; beat 2 minutes more at medium speed. Fill the muffin cups two-thirds full.

Bake for 15 to 20 minutes, until a toothpick inserted in the center comes out clean. Remove from the pans and cool completely on wire racks.

Place the thawed whipped topping in a large bowl; fold in the remaining candy. Frost the cooled cupcakes and store in the refrigerator until ready to serve.

A CHOICE INGREDIENT

I remember lard was the choice ingredient in all foods baked, fried, or needing some shortening as I was growing up.

My grandfather butchered the hogs, my grandmother rendered the lard, and we ate the cracklings in our bowl of fresh cooked beans (*frijoles de la olla*), with a side of fresh tortillas, also made with lard. Grandmother put the lard in clean, sterile jars, and then sealed it so that she could use it as she needed.

As I got older, my mother cooked all things with lard. I remember the familiar green-and-white package brought from the store (*manteca*, it said on the side) and as our family grew, we continued to use the little bucket with lard in it.

When Mother made fresh tortillas, she taught us to spread a little lard on one, sprinkle a little salt, and that was our "buttered" tortilla.

My Aunt Kadie made the best pies in the world, with the flakiest crusts, and she said only use lard for the crust, not shortening, as the shortening would "toughen" the dough.

Today, being a modern, health-conscious woman, I use only shortening for baking, or cooking spray and olive oil for frying. But I remember how good everything tasted when I was young and I ate everything with lard!

Terry Ardolf, Fairmont, Minnesota

FUDGE CAKE

This is your go-to chocolate layer cake for birthdays. It's what they expect; it's what they want; it's what they'll love and ask for every year. Decorate the top with sprinkles, jimmies, nonpareils, gumdrops, chocolate chips—the sky's the limit! Serves 12

½ cup lard, softened, plus more
for greasing the pans

2¼ cups all-purpose unbleached flour,
plus more for dusting the pans

1 teaspoon baking soda

1 teaspoon baking powder

½ teaspoon salt

1½ cups granulated sugar

1 teaspoon vanilla extract

2 eggs, well beaten

½ cup unsweetened cocoa

⅓ cup hot water

1 cup buttermilk

FROSTING

1½ cups semisweet chocolate chips

1 cup unsalted butter, softened

¼ cup lard, softened

1 cup confectioners' sugar

¾ cup cocoa

⅛ teaspoon salt

¾ cup light corn syrup

1 teaspoon vanilla extract

Preheat the oven to 350°F. Generously grease two 9-inch or three 8-inch cake pans with lard; dust lightly with flour and set aside.

In a medium bowl, sift together the flour, baking soda, baking powder, and salt; set aside. In a large bowl, cream together the lard and granulated sugar using an electric mixer on low speed. Add the vanilla and eggs; beat on medium speed until light and fluffy.

In a small bowl, whisk together the cocoa and hot water to form a smooth paste; set aside. Alternately add the flour mixture and buttermilk to the lard mixture, beating well after each addition. Add the cocoa mixture and beat well.

Divide the batter evenly among the prepared pans and bake for 30 to 35 minutes, until the cake springs back after gently pressing with a finger. Cool in the pans on a wire rack for 10 minutes, then turn out to cool completely.

To prepare the frosting, place the chocolate chips in a double boiler or microwave-safe bowl. Heat until melted; stir until smooth. Set aside to cool slightly.

In a food processor fitted with a metal blade, process the butter, lard, confectioners' sugar, cocoa, and salt for 30 seconds until smooth, scraping down the bowl as needed. Add the corn syrup and vanilla and pulse until just combined, 5 to 10 seconds.

Add the melted chocolate and process until creamy and smooth, 10 to 15 seconds.

To frost the cake, place one cake layer on a cake stand and frost, using an offset spatula. Position the second layer atop the first and repeat.

CHOCOLATE KRAUT CAKE

Cake and fermented cabbage? Indeed. The origin of this recipe can be traced to the 1960s when the USDA Surplus Committee requested (specifically to school lunchroom managers) ways to use up a large quantity of stockpiled canned sauerkraut. Mrs. Geraldine Timms, supervisor of the lunchroom at Waller High School in Chicago, came up with this cake, which became all the rage. It's very moist and without even a hint of sauerkraut flavor—you'll swear you're eating coconut.
Serves 12

⅔ cup lard, softened, plus more for greasing the pan

2½ cups all-purpose unbleached flour, plus more for the pan

1 teaspoon baking soda

1 teaspoon baking powder

1½ cups sugar

3 eggs

1¼ teaspoons vanilla extract

¼ teaspoon salt

½ cup unsweetened cocoa

1 cup water

1 cup chopped sauerkraut, drained and rinsed

1 (21-ounce) can cherry pie filling (optional)

Preheat the oven to 375°F. Grease and flour a bundt or angel food cake pan with lard; set aside.

In a large mixing bowl, sift together the flour, baking soda, and baking powder; set aside.

In a medium mixing bowl, using an electric mixer on low speed, cream together the sugar and lard. Add the eggs, vanilla, salt, and cocoa; mix well. Alternately add the flour mixture and the water to the creamed mixture, beating well after each addition. Stir in the sauerkraut and mix well. Pour the batter into the prepared pan.

Bake for 45 to 50 minutes, until the cake springs back after gently pressing with a finger. Cool completely on a wire rack.

To serve, invert the cake on a serving stand and spread the pie filling, if using, over the top.

NO-ICING CHOCOLATE CHIP CAKE

Using dates in baked goods, particularly cakes, is a very old practice. The dates extend the cake's shelf life, with it becoming moister each day that it sits covered (think of fruitcakes and their indefinite shelf life). Soaking the dates in baking soda and boiling water causes them to swell up and macerate, making them easier to blend throughout the cake; the baking soda essentially tenderizes the date's skin and makes the fruit more digestible. Serve this cake in the afternoon as a light snack. Serves 12

1 cup lard, softened, plus more for greasing the pan

1 cup chopped dates

1 cup plus 3 tablespoons hot water

1 teaspoon baking soda

1 cup sugar

2 eggs, beaten

2 cups all-purpose unbleached flour

½ teaspoon salt

1 tablespoon unsweetened cocoa

1 teaspoon vanilla extract

1 cup semisweet chocolate chips

½ cup chopped pecans

Preheat the oven to 350°F. Grease a 13 by 9-inch baking pan with lard and set aside.

Place the dates in a large bowl and cover with 1 cup hot water. In a small bowl, dissolve the baking soda in the remaining 3 tablespoons hot water; add to the dates. Set aside.

In a large bowl, using an electric mixer on low speed, cream together the sugar and lard. Add the eggs, flour, salt, cocoa, and vanilla; beat well. Stir in the date mixture and ½ cup chocolate chips.

Pour the batter into the prepared pan. Sprinkle the remaining ½ cup chocolate chips and the pecans on top.

Bake for 40 minutes, until the cake begins to pull away from the sides of the pan and a toothpick inserted in the center comes out clean. Cool completely on a wire rack.

COCOA DIVINITY CAKE

Cocoa divinity cake is an old recipe, probably found in the handwritten recipe books of our ancestors. It's similar to the popular red velvet cake and gets its soft, delicate chocolate flavor and texture from buttermilk. "Divinity" refers to the white icing that will harden as it dries. The red glow of the cake's interior is what makes it dramatic and fun, and a perennial crowd-pleaser. **Serves 12**

⅔ cup lard, softened, plus more for greasing the pans

2 cups all-purpose unbleached flour, plus more for dusting the pans

1½ cups granulated sugar

1¼ teaspoons baking soda

1 teaspoon salt

6 tablespoons unsweetened cocoa

1 cup buttermilk

2 eggs

¼ teaspoon red food coloring

FROSTING

¼ cup salted butter

2 cups confectioners' sugar

2 tablespoons heavy cream

1 teaspoon lard, melted

1½ teaspoons vanilla extract

1 teaspoon hot water

Preheat the oven to 350°F. Generously grease two 9-inch cake pans with lard; dust lightly with flour and set aside.

In a large bowl, sift together the flour, granulated sugar, baking soda, salt, and cocoa. In a separate bowl, using an electric mixer on low speed, cream together the lard and buttermilk; add to the sifted ingredients and beat for 2 minutes. Add the eggs and food coloring; beat for 2 minutes longer. Pour the batter evenly into the prepared pans.

Bake for 30 to 35 minutes, until the cake springs back after gently pressing with a finger. Cool in the pans on a wire rack for 10 minutes, then turn out to cool completely.

To prepare the frosting, melt the butter in a saucepan over low heat; remove from the heat. Blend in the confectioners' sugar, heavy cream, lard, vanilla, and hot water; whisk until smooth. Remove from the heat to cool slightly.

To frost the cake, place one cake layer on a cake stand and frost, using an offset spatula. Position the second layer atop the first and repeat.

COFFEE CRUNCH KUCHEN

Kuchen, the German word for "cake," is used to describe an infinite number of sweet desserts or pastries. Kuchen desserts came to America with German immigrants and are popular in areas of German settlement such as North Dakota, South Dakota, Indiana, Minnesota, and Wisconsin. In 2000, a kuchen was even designated the state dessert of South Dakota. Make this easy coffee cake version (with real coffee and extra fiber) for a breakfast or brunch. Serves **12**

½ cup lard, softened, plus more for greasing the pan

2¼ cups all-purpose unbleached flour, plus more for dusting the pan

2 cups brown sugar, packed

1 cup bran flakes cereal

3 teaspoons baking powder

Pinch of salt

½ cup salted butter, softened

½ cup brewed coffee, cold

½ cup evaporated milk

⅛ teaspoon baking soda

2 eggs, beaten

1 teaspoon cinnamon

½ cup chopped pecans

Preheat the oven to 375°F. Grease a 13 by 9-inch baking dish with lard; dust lightly with flour and set aside.

In a large bowl, mix together the flour, brown sugar, bran flakes, baking powder, and salt. Using a pastry blender, cut in the lard and butter until the mixture resembles coarse crumbs. Set aside 1 cup of the mixture to use later as a topping.

Combine the coffee, evaporated milk, and baking soda. Add to the remaining flour mixture and mix thoroughly. Stir in the eggs. Pour the batter into the prepared baking dish.

Add the cinnamon to the reserved topping and mix well; sprinkle evenly over the batter and top with the pecans.

Bake for 30 to 35 minutes, until a toothpick inserted in the center comes out clean. Serve warm.

BLACKBERRY CAKE

Most blackberry cakes are made with jam or preserves . . . not this one. Use the whole, ripe, plump blackberries, bursting with juice, that you just picked from the thicket in the yard. Gently muddle the fruit before adding it to the batter to release more of its juices. The icing is like fondant and will give you the impression that you're eating something very, very special indeed.   Serves 10 to 12

⅓ cup lard, softened, plus more for greasing the pans

2 cups cake flour, plus more for dusting the pans

3⅓ cups sugar

3 eggs, beaten

1 cup buttermilk

1 cup ripe soft blackberries, gently muddled

1 teaspoon baking soda

1 teaspoon baking powder

1 teaspoon ground cloves

1 teaspoon allspice

1 teaspoon cinnamon

1 cup chopped walnuts

1 cup milk

3 tablespoons salted butter

Preheat the oven to 350°F. Grease three 8-inch cake pans with lard; lightly dust with flour and set aside.

In a large bowl, using an electric mixer on low speed, cream 1⅓ cups sugar with the lard; add the eggs, buttermilk, and blackberries. In a separate bowl, combine the flour, baking soda, baking powder, cloves, allspice, and cinnamon. Add the dry mixture to the creamed mixture and beat well. Fold in the nuts and mix well.

Pour the batter into the prepared cake pans. Bake for 25 minutes, until the cake springs back after gently pressing with a finger. Cool for 10 minutes on a wire rack; then turn out to cool completely.

To make the frosting, combine the remaining 2 cups sugar, the milk, and butter in a medium saucepan over medium heat. Using a candy thermometer, cook to the soft ball stage (235° to 240°F). Remove the pan from the heat and beat on medium speed until thick; set aside to cool.

To frost the cake, place one cake layer on a cake stand and frost, using an offset spatula. Position the second layer atop the first and repeat. Repeat with the third layer and smooth the frosting over all.

LARD REALLY IS BETTER
Sizzling side pork, fresh from the back room (natural refrigeration) in my grandparents' cottonwood log house, woke me on cold North Dakota mornings. They lived on the school side of the river, so I lived with them when ice on the river was too thin or breaking up in the spring.

The lard they rendered and used may be the reason my pie crusts and biscuits never turned out as good as Mom's and Grandma's. I always thought that butter was healthier than oleo, but I never dreamed that lard had less saturated fat and cholesterol than butter—and no trans fats. I certainly will go back to using it in my pie crusts.

It is amazing how many things were as good or better for you back then. I always wondered how the fat could be so bad for you when my grandmother cooked that way and lived to be ninety-six years old. She was in her own home, independent, at age ninety.

Jo Lee T. Riley, Culver, Oregon

GEORGIA PEACH CAKE

This old-fashioned, unique meringue-topped cake is reminiscent of the 1950s when housewives prided themselves on a remarkable cake. If you've never made meringue, don't worry—it's not hard. This is the easiest of the three meringue methods: Just beat the egg whites until they coagulate and form soft peaks, then add the sugar slowly until the mixture has grown in volume but is still soft, airy, and light. The meringue should stand up when the beaters are lifted.
Serves 10 to 12

½ cup lard, softened, plus more for greasing the pans

2 cups cake flour

4 teaspoons baking powder

1¾ cups sugar

4 eggs, separated, beaten, plus 1 egg white

¾ cup milk

1½ teaspoons vanilla extract

¼ teaspoon almond extract

2 cups peaches, crushed and drained, syrup reserved

¾ cup heavy syrup (from canned peaches)

6 large marshmallows, quartered

Preheat the oven to 350°F. Grease two 9-inch cake pans with lard and set aside.

Sift the flour; measure 2 cups and sift three more times, adding the baking powder on the last sifting. Set aside.

In a large bowl, using an electric mixer on low speed, cream the lard; gradually add 1 cup sugar and beat until light and fluffy. Add the 4 beaten egg yolks.

Alternately add the flour mixture and the milk to the creamed mixture, beating just enough to make a smooth batter. Mix in 1 teaspoon vanilla.

Pour the batter evenly into the prepared cake pans. Bake for 25 minutes, until the cake springs back after gently pressing with a finger. Remove the cakes from the oven and reduce the oven temperature to 325°F. Invert the cakes onto a wire rack to cool completely. When cool, set the cakes on a baking sheet.

In a large bowl, using an electric mixer on high speed, beat the 4 egg whites until soft peaks form. Fold in ½ cup sugar slowly and beat a few minutes longer. Add the almond extract. Pile the meringue lightly over the cooled cake layers and bake for 15 to 20 minutes, until lightly browned; cool. Place one cake layer on a cake stand and spread the peaches over the top. Top with the remaining layer.

In a saucepan over medium heat, heat the heavy syrup and the remaining ¼ cup sugar until thick. Add the marshmallows and stir; remove from the heat and allow the mixture to cool slightly.

In a medium bowl, beat the remaining egg white until stiff; gradually pour the warm syrup mixture over the egg white, beating all the time. Beat in the remaining ½ teaspoon vanilla. Serve the syrup in a pitcher alongside the cake for guests to pour themselves.

MAKE A DELICIOUS CAKE

I have been cooking with lard only for the last couple of years, after being brought up in a home where we made our own lard every winter. We always used it for pie crust.

I use cast-iron skillets and use the lard for most frying, and it does not take much to fry things golden brown. Just a few drops in an iron skillet makes wonderful toasted cheese sandwiches.

I buy the deodorized lard from the Hearthside Country Store in Sabetha, Kansas; it is wonderful. I am including a recipe I received from a friend whose mother made this cake all the time, and it is very good.

Irene L. Yoesel, via e-mail

LARD CHOCOLATE CAKE Serves 10 to 12

½ cup lard, plus more for greasing the pan

2¼ cups all-purpose unbleached flour, plus more for dusting the pan

½ cup unsweetened cocoa

½ teaspoon salt

1⅛ cups cold water

3 egg whites

1¾ cups sugar

1 teaspoon vanilla extract

1½ teaspoons baking soda

2 tablespoons boiling water

Preheat the oven to 350°F. Grease with lard and flour a 9 by 13-inch cake pan; set aside.

Mix together the cocoa, salt, and ⅓ cup of the cold water; set aside. Beat the egg whites and ¾ cup sugar until stiff peaks form; set aside.

Cream together the remaining 1 cup sugar, the lard, and vanilla. Add the flour alternately with the remaining 1 cup cold water to the creamed mixture. Add the cocoa mixture and blend.

Mix the baking soda into the boiling water; add to the batter. Blend well; fold in the beaten egg whites until blended in.

Bake for 30 minutes, or until the cake tests done.

NOTE: This might sound complicated, but it goes together very easily and is very good.

RHUBARB PUDDING CAKE

This cake is a smart and delicious way to use all the rhubarb come late spring, when your plants are sending up lots of stalks. The tart rhubarb will gently meld with the sweet batter and form a puddinglike consistency. To tame the sour flavor of rhubarb, before dicing the stalks, soak them in a gallon of cold water for 20 minutes; rinse and proceed. Serve this cake with a pour of heavy cream over the top. **Serves 8 to 10**

⅓ cup lard, softened, plus
more for greasing the pan

4 cups chopped fresh rhubarb

1⅔ cups sugar

¾ cup water

1 cup all-purpose unbleached flour

1 teaspoon baking powder

¼ teaspoon salt

1 egg

⅔ cup milk

½ teaspoon vanilla extract

Preheat the oven to 350°F. Grease a 9-inch cake pan with lard and set aside.

In a medium saucepan, combine the rhubarb, 1 cup sugar, and the water. Heat over medium-high heat until boiling; reduce the heat to low and simmer, stirring frequently, until the rhubarb is tender, about 20 minutes. Remove from the heat and keep warm until needed.

In a large bowl, sift together the flour, baking powder, and salt. In a separate bowl, using an electric mixer on low speed, cream together the lard and the remaining ⅔ cup sugar; add the egg and beat until light. In a small bowl, combine the milk and vanilla. Alternately add the flour mixture and the milk mixture to the creamed mixture, stirring until smooth after each addition.

Pour the batter into the prepared pan. Spoon the rhubarb mixture carefully over the batter in the pan.

Bake for 35 to 40 minutes, until a toothpick inserted in the center comes out clean. Serve warm.

SOUTHERN GINGERBREAD
with APRICOT CREAM FILLING

Gingerbread was brought to Sweden during the thirteenth century by German immigrants, and soon Swedish nuns were using it to ease indigestion. This soft, moist, and spicy cake now associated with Christmas is made "southern" here with the addition of whipped cream and apricots, making it delicious any time of the year. If you're a super fan of ginger and would like a more pronounced ginger flavor, substitute the 2 teaspoons ground ginger with 3 tablespoons peeled and grated fresh ginger plus 3 tablespoons minced crystallized ginger. **Serves 10**

1 cup coarsely chopped dried apricots

¾ cup lard, melted, plus more
for greasing the pan

2½ cups all-purpose unbleached flour,
plus more for dusting the pan

2 eggs, beaten

¾ cup brown sugar, packed

¾ cup mild molasses

2 teaspoons baking powder

½ teaspoon baking soda

½ teaspoon plus a pinch of salt

2 teaspoons ground ginger

1½ teaspoons cinnamon

½ teaspoon nutmeg

½ teaspoon ground cloves

1 cup boiling water

1 cup heavy cream

3 tablespoons granulated sugar

Place the dried apricots in a small saucepan and cover with water. Heat over medium heat and simmer, uncovered, for about 20 minutes, until the apricots are plump; drain. Set aside to cool.

Preheat the oven to 350°F. Grease a 9-inch square baking pan with lard; lightly dust with flour and set aside.

In a large bowl, combine the eggs, brown sugar, molasses, and lard. In a separate bowl, sift together the flour, baking powder, baking soda, ½ teaspoon salt, the ginger, cinnamon, nutmeg, and cloves; add to the molasses mixture and stir. Blend in the boiling water.

Pour the batter into the prepared cake pans and bake for 30 to 40 minutes, until the cake starts to pull away from the sides of the pan and springs back after gently pressing with a finger. Cool completely on a wire rack.

Pour the cream into a large bowl. Using an electric mixer on high speed, beat until stiff peaks form. In a separate bowl, combine the apricots, granulated sugar, and a pinch of salt. Fold in the whipped cream.

Cut the cake into squares and top with a dollop of the apricot whipped cream. Serve immediately.

WORLD WAR II CAKE
with BASIC BUTTERCREAM FROSTING

During World War II, cooks were forced to do a lot of improvising due to rationing. Certain staples such as eggs, butter, and sugar just weren't available. Eggs were rationed (and scarce), so this recipe uses none—it's one of those improvisations that defined an era. Without doubt, this cake was toted to a USO dance by a young woman in a polka-dot dress and pearls. Serves 8 to 10

1 cup dark brown sugar, packed

1½ cups plus 2 teaspoons water

⅓ cup lard, plus more for greasing the pan

1 to 2 cups raisins

1 teaspoon cinnamon

½ teaspoon nutmeg

½ teaspoon cloves

2 cups all-purpose unbleached flour, sifted, plus more for dusting the pan

1 teaspoon salt

1 teaspoon baking soda

1 teaspoon baking powder

BASIC BUTTERCREAM FROSTING

2½ tablespoons salted butter, softened

1 cup confectioners' sugar

1 tablespoon milk

½ teaspoon vanilla extract

¼ cup chopped walnuts (optional)

In a saucepan, combine the brown sugar, 1½ cups water, the lard, raisins, cinnamon, nutmeg, and cloves. Heat to boiling and continue boiling for 3 minutes. Remove from the heat and set aside to cool. Once cool, transfer to a large bowl.

Preheat the oven to 325°F. Lightly grease an 8-inch square cake pan with lard; lightly dust with flour and set aside.

Dissolve the salt and baking soda in the remaining 2 teaspoons water; stir into the raisin mixture. Add the flour and baking powder and mix well.

Pour the batter into the prepared pan and bake for 45 to 50 minutes, until the cake springs back after being gently pressed with a finger. Leave the cake in the pan and cool completely on a wire rack.

To prepare the frosting, in a large bowl, cream the butter, using a hand mixer on low speed. Add the confectioners' sugar, milk, and vanilla and beat until smooth and no lumps remain. Fold in the walnuts, if using. Spread the frosting on the cooled cake, using an offset spatula.

BLACK WALNUT CAKE

If you've never tasted black walnuts, be prepared for something much different than the common, mild-tasting English walnut. The nutmeats are distinctively robust. Black walnuts are a traditional ingredient in vintage recipes for baked goods and ice cream because the trees were commonplace on farms. Since extracting the kernel from the fruit is beyond difficult (old-timers usually ran over them with the truck), black walnuts tend to be pricey. Look for them in the baking supplies aisle in better grocery stores. **Serves 12**

¼ cup lard, softened, plus more for greasing the pan(s)

2 cups all-purpose unbleached flour, plus more for dusting the pan(s)

¼ cup salted butter, softened

1¼ cups sugar

2 eggs

2 teaspoons baking powder

½ teaspoon salt

¾ cup milk

1 teaspoon vanilla extract

1 cup chopped black walnuts

Vanilla or black walnut ice cream and/or pure maple syrup, for serving

Preheat the oven to 350°F. Grease one 8 by 12-inch loaf pan or two 8-inch round layer cake pans with lard; lightly dust with flour and set aside.

In a large bowl, using an electric mixer on low speed, cream the butter with the lard and sugar. Add the eggs and blend well; set aside. In a separate bowl, sift the flour with the baking powder and salt. Alternately add the flour mixture and the milk to the creamed mixture, beating well after each addition. Stir in the vanilla and black walnuts.

Spread the batter evenly into the prepared pan(s). Bake for 30 to 45 minutes, until the cake starts to pull away from the sides of the pan and springs back after gently pressing with a finger. Turn out onto wire racks to cool completely. Serve with vanilla or black walnut ice cream and/or a pour of pure maple syrup.

PLAIN CAKE MIX

Before cake mixes were common on grocery store shelves, cooks used to mix up their own for ease and convenience. When the need or desire for a cake arose, this versatile mix came in handy. Substitute different flavored extracts for variation, and prepare your favorite frosting to spread on top. **Serves 8**

8 cups all-purpose unbleached flour

3 tablespoons baking powder

1½ teaspoons salt

2 cups lard, softened, plus more for greasing the pan

2½ cups sugar

PLAIN CAKE Serves 8 to 10

1 bag Plain Cake Mix

Scant cup of milk

2 eggs, beaten

1 teaspoon lemon extract

In a very large bowl, sift the flour once; measure 8 cups. Add the baking powder and salt and sift an additional two times.

In a separate very large bowl, using an electric mixer on low speed, cream the lard until soft; add the sugar gradually and continue beating. Blend in the sifted ingredients until the mixture resembles fine crumbs. Divide the mixture into thirds and store in individual zip-top plastic bags in a cool, dry place or in the refrigerator until needed.

To make Plain Cake, preheat the oven to 375°F. Grease two 9-inch layer cake pans or one 11 by 14-inch loaf pan with lard. Set aside.

In a large bowl, place the mix. Use a fork to break up any clumps. Add the milk, eggs, and lemon extract; beat well with an electric mixer on medium-low speed.

Pour the batter into the prepared pan(s) and bake for 25 to 30 minutes, until the cake starts to pull away from the sides of the pan and springs back after being gently pressed with a finger. Cool on wire racks. Serve the cake plain or frosted.

POPPY SEED CAKE

This cake is a vision—strikingly white, chock-full of poppy seeds, with white, shimmering frosting. Soaking the seeds beforehand softens them and makes them more digestible—don't skip this step! Serves 10 to 12

CAKE

½ cup poppy seeds

1 cup milk

½ cup lard, softened, plus more for greasing the pans

1½ cups sugar

1 egg

2 egg whites

1 teaspoon vanilla extract

2 cups sifted all-purpose unbleached flour

2 teaspoons baking powder

½ teaspoon salt

FILLING

1 egg yolk

½ cup milk

½ cup sugar

1 teaspoon cornstarch

½ teaspoon vanilla extract

½ cup chopped pecans

FROSTING

2 egg whites

¾ cup sugar

¼ cup water

Pinch of salt

Place the poppy seeds in a small bowl; add the milk and soak for at least 30 minutes or overnight.

Preheat the oven to 350°F. Grease the bottoms of two 8-inch round cake pans with lard. Cut wax paper to fit the pan bottoms; place in the pans and grease the wax paper with lard. Set aside.

To make the cake, in a large bowl, using an electric mixer on low speed, cream together the sugar and lard. Add the egg, egg whites, the poppy seed mixture, vanilla, flour, baking powder, and salt; beat until smooth.

Pour the batter into the prepared pans and bake for 40 minutes, until the cake springs back after being gently pressed with a finger. Check frequently near the end of the baking time for doneness. Cool completely on a wire rack.

To make the filling, in a saucepan over low heat, combine the egg yolk, milk, sugar, and cornstarch; cook until the mixture thickens, about 5 minutes, stirring frequently. Remove the pan from the heat, and stir in the vanilla and pecans. Let cool.

To make the frosting, using an electric mixer on high speed, beat the egg whites until stiff peaks form. In a saucepan, combine the sugar, water, and a pinch of salt. Using a candy thermometer, cook until it reaches the thread stage (230° to 235°F). Pour over the beaten egg whites; beat until the mixture stands in peaks.

To finish the cake, place one cake layer on a cake stand. Spread the filling mixture on top. Place the second layer on top of the first and frost the entire cake, using an offset spatula.

STRAWBERRY SODA POP CAKE

This cake came about during the 1950s when soda pop (just "pop" in the Midwest) was the occasional special treat rather than an everyday beverage. Substitute with your favorite pop— grape, orange, lemon-lime—to create variations. If you're a fan of jam cake, spread strawberry jam (or grape, orange marmalade, or lemon curd, respectively) between the layers instead of the frosting. **Serves 8 to 10**

¾ cup lard, softened, plus more for greasing the pans

3 cups all-purpose unbleached flour, plus more for dusting the pans

2 cups granulated sugar

2 teaspoons baking powder

½ teaspoon salt

1 (7-ounce) bottle strawberry soda pop

1 cup chopped walnuts or pecans

5 egg whites, stiffly beaten

FROSTING

2 tablespoons lard, softened

Pinch of salt

2 cups confectioners' sugar

1 (12-ounce) bottle or can strawberry soda pop

Preheat the oven to 350°F. Generously grease two 9-inch cake pans with lard; dust lightly with flour and set aside.

In a large bowl, cream together the lard and granulated sugar with an electric mixer on low speed. In a separate bowl, sift together the flour, baking powder, and salt. Alternately add the flour mixture and the strawberry pop to the creamed mixture, beating well after each addition. Stir in the nuts; fold in the egg whites.

Distribute the batter evenly between the cake pans and bake 30 to 40 minutes, until a toothpick inserted in the center comes out clean. Cool in the pans for 10 minutes, then turn out onto wire racks to cool completely.

To prepare the frosting, combine the lard, salt, confectioners' sugar, and just enough strawberry pop to moisten the mixture; blend well until smooth and creamy. To frost the cake, place one cake layer on a cake stand and frost, using an offset spatula. Position the second layer atop the first and repeat.

RUTH'S RAISIN CAKE

Ruth was a woman of few words, and she liked her recipes to reflect her personality. Her simple, unadorned cake has comparatively few steps and is easy to bring together when you're short on time. Serve with a scoop of rum–raisin or cinnamon ice cream, or a pour of heavy cream.
Serves 10 to 12

1½ cups raisins

1½ cups boiling water

¼ cup lard, softened, plus more for greasing the pan

1½ cups all-purpose unbleached flour, plus more for dusting the pan

¾ cup sugar

1 egg, beaten

1 teaspoon baking soda

1 teaspoon nutmeg

1 teaspoon cinnamon

½ teaspoon salt

Place the raisins in a saucepan. Pour the boiling water over them and turn the heat to medium; simmer for 20 minutes. Remove from the heat and cool.

Preheat the oven to 350°F. Grease a tube or loaf pan with lard; lightly dust with flour and set aside.

In a large bowl, using an electric mixer on low speed, cream together the lard and sugar; add the egg and beat until smooth. Set aside.

In a large bowl, sift together the flour, baking soda, nutmeg, cinnamon, and salt; repeat two more times.

Alternately add the cooled raisin mixture and the flour mixture to the creamed mixture, mixing thoroughly by hand after each addition.

Pour the batter into the prepared pan and bake for 40 minutes, until the cake springs back after gently pressed with a finger. Cool on a wire rack for 5 minutes, then invert to cool completely.

BUTTERMILK POUND CAKE

The definition of pound cake is a cake traditionally made with a pound of each of four ingredients—flour, butter, eggs, and sugar—and involves more steps than most cooks care to complete. Many nonconforming variations exist—such as this easy one-bowl cake with a citrus glaze—yet the name still applies. This cake is dense like a pound cake but with the tang of buttermilk and the absence of butter (lard in its place). Substitute almond or vanilla extract for the lemon extract for variation. Pound cake will keep for up to 5 days, wrapped tightly, in the refrigerator. **Serves 10 to 12**

**1 cup lard, softened, plus more
for greasing the pan**

**3 cups sifted all-purpose unbleached
flour, plus more for dusting the pan**

2 cups granulated sugar

4 eggs

1 cup buttermilk

2 tablespoons lemon extract

½ teaspoon baking soda

½ teaspoon salt

½ teaspoon baking powder

GLAZE

2 cups sifted confectioners' sugar

2 tablespoons fresh orange juice

2 tablespoons fresh lemon juice

Preheat the oven to 300°F. Grease a tube pan with lard; lightly dust with flour and set aside.

In a large bowl, using an electric mixer on low speed, cream together the lard and granulated sugar; add the eggs, buttermilk, and lemon extract and mix well. Add the flour, baking soda, salt, and baking powder; beat on medium speed for 3 minutes. Pour the batter into the prepared pan. Bake for 1 hour, until golden brown and the cake springs back when pressed gently with a finger. Cool on a wire rack; keep the oven turned on.

To make the glaze, in a medium bowl, combine the confectioners' sugar, orange juice, and lemon juice; beat until smooth.

Run a knife around the edge of the cake pan and pour the glaze all around the edge. Return the cake to the oven for 3 minutes. Remove the cake from the pan at once by inverting onto a serving plate. Cool.

Fried Fruit Pies, page 154

Cherry Pie, page 160

Pineapple–Coconut Cupcakes, page 169

Fudge Cake, page 172

Strawberry Soda Pop Cake, page 192

Sunshine Shortcake, page 195

Easy Cocoa Pudding, page 210

Apple Pizza, page 219

SUNSHINE SHORTCAKE

This is a favorite dessert in the sunny South, where peaches are a point of pride. Ripe, juicy farm-stand peaches work best in this recipe, but in lieu of that seasonal sight, use good-quality canned peaches—or better yet, your own canned peaches from last summer. Finishing it with a few blueberries also adds some nice color if you like.   **Serves 8 to 10**

½ cup lard, softened, plus more
for greasing the pans

1¾ cups all-purpose unbleached flour,
plus more for dusting the pans

⅔ cup sugar

2 eggs, separated

1 teaspoon grated orange zest

2 teaspoons baking powder

¾ teaspoon salt

½ cup fresh orange juice

TOPPING
2 cups whipped cream
(about 1 cup liquid)

2 cups fresh or canned
peach slices, drained

Preheat the oven to 375°F. Grease two 8-inch layer cake pans with lard; dust lightly with flour and set aside.

In a large bowl, cream together the lard and sugar; beat in the egg yolks. Stir in the orange zest. In a separate bowl, sift together the flour, baking powder, and salt.

Alternately add the flour mixture and the orange juice to the creamed mixture, beating well after each addition. In a separate bowl, beat the egg whites until stiff peaks form. Fold into the batter. Pour the batter into the prepared cake pans.

Bake for 20 minutes, until a toothpick inserted in the center comes out clean. Let cool in the pans for 5 minutes, then turn out onto a wire rack to cool completely.

Just before serving, place one cake layer on a cake stand. Spread half the whipped cream on top, then half the peaches. Place the second layer on top and repeat. Serve immediately.

BROWN SUGAR MERINGUE SPICE CAKE

This fragrant spice cake is just perfect for an autumn or winter dinner party where you've been asked to bring the dessert and you want to show up with something besides the usual fare. The meringue topping bakes into a thin, crispy crust with a soft, chewy meringue beneath it, perched atop a brown sugar-and-spice cake. When sliced, the meringue will crack and meld with the cake. Serves 8 to 10

½ cup lard, softened, plus more for greasing the pan

1⅓ cups sifted all-purpose unbleached flour, plus more for dusting the pan

½ teaspoon baking soda

½ teaspoon baking powder

½ teaspoon cloves

½ teaspoon cinnamon

¼ teaspoon salt

1½ cups brown sugar, packed

2 eggs

½ cup buttermilk

Pinch of cream of tartar

½ cup chopped pecans

Preheat the oven to 350°F. Grease a 9 by 5-inch loaf pan with lard; lightly dust with flour and set aside.

In a large bowl, sift together the sifted flour, baking soda, baking powder, cloves, cinnamon, and salt. Set aside.

In a separate bowl, using an electric mixer on low speed, cream the lard until soft; gradually add 1 cup brown sugar and continue to cream until the mixture is light and fluffy.

In another bowl, beat 1 egg and 1 egg yolk on medium-high speed until light; add to the creamed mixture and beat thoroughly. Alternately add the flour mixture and the buttermilk to the creamed mixture, beating well after each addition. Pour the batter into the prepared pan.

Beat the remaining egg white and the cream of tartar on high speed until frothy. Gradually add the remaining ½ cup brown sugar and continue to beat on high speed until stiff peaks form, about 5 minutes. Fold in the pecans. Spread the meringue over the cake batter in the pan; use the back of a spoon to make soft peaks and valleys.

Bake for 50 minutes, until the cake starts to pull away from the sides of the pan and the meringue is lightly browned and crisp. Cool on a wire rack. Run a knife around the edge of the cake in the pan and, using an offset spatula, lift it out onto a serving platter. Serve at room temperature.

ONE CAVEAT I would suggest that it be made clear that this type of lard does not refer to the pasteurized, homogenized, sanitized white stuff from the supermarket. In California, we can buy excellent lard from Mexican markets. It is known as *manteca* and is tan in color with a wonderful flavor. Bacon fat from nonchemically cured bacon is reasonably good, also.

I save bacon grease for cooking refried beans, eggs, French toast, and more.

Larry M. Jones, Berkeley, California

CRANBERRY UPSIDE-DOWN CAKE

This easy, yet beautiful—and delicious—upside-down cake is ratcheted up a notch with the addition of hard sauce. Hard sauce is a sweet, rich sauce made with butter and booze, meant to be spooned onto warm pies, bread puddings, cobblers, and crisps—and in this case, upside-down cake. Since its base is butter, once it meets the warm cake, it'll melt and ooze down the sides, creating an irresistible concoction. **Serves 10 to 12**

3 tablespoons salted butter

1½ cups granulated sugar

2 cups fresh cranberries, washed and dried

¼ cup lard, softened

1 egg, well beaten

1½ cups all-purpose unbleached flour

1½ teaspoons baking powder

¼ teaspoon salt

½ cup milk

1 teaspoon vanilla extract

HARD SAUCE

½ cup salted butter, softened

1½ cups confectioners' sugar

2 tablespoons rum, brandy, whiskey, or sherry

Preheat the oven to 350°F.

In a large ovenproof skillet over medium heat, melt the butter and 1 cup granulated sugar; add the cranberries and stir. Cook over low heat for 5 minutes, stirring frequently. Remove from the heat and set aside.

In a medium bowl, using an electric mixer on low speed, cream the lard and the remaining ½ cup granulated sugar; add the egg. In a separate bowl, sift together the flour, baking powder, and salt. Alternately add the flour mixture and the milk to the creamed mixture, beating well after each addition. Stir in the vanilla.

Pour the batter over the cranberry mixture in the skillet.

Bake for 35 minutes, until the cake is golden brown. Invert the cake on a serving platter.

To make the hard sauce, using an electric mixer on medium speed, beat the butter until fluffy. Gradually add the confectioners' sugar, beating until thoroughly moistened. Add the rum and beat until smooth and no lumps remain. Serve the cake warm with the hard sauce.

CHERISHED COOKBOOK My grandma used lard for everything. My most cherished possession passed down from her is an old handwritten cookbook made by my great-grandma between 1890 and 1920. Amounts are written as "lard the size of a hen's egg" or "the size of a walnut."

Of all the recipes, my favorite was my grandma's pancakes. After mixing the batter a bit thinner than the puffy ones of today, she'd fry them in lard in a cast-iron skillet until the edges were dark and crispy, and then serve them with homemade syrup.

Nothing can compare to that flavor, and I still make my pancakes the same way.

Joyce Keeling, Springfield, Missouri

RHUBARB TOPSY-TURVY

Though rhubarb is usually considered a vegetable, in 1947 a New York court decided that since it was primarily used as a fruit (in pies and desserts), it was to be counted as such for the purposes of regulations and duties. Most commonly used in pies, rhubarb came to be known as "pie plant" in the latter nineteenth century and is still referred to as such by old-timers. Serve this inside-out pie, if you will, warm with whipped cream. Serves 12

½ cup lard, softened, plus more for greasing the pan

3 cups diced rhubarb

12 large marshmallows

1¾ cups sugar

2 eggs, beaten

1¾ cups all-purpose unbleached flour

¼ teaspoon salt

3 tablespoons baking powder

½ cup milk

Preheat the oven to 350°F. Generously grease a 13 by 9-inch glass baking dish with lard.

Place the rhubarb in the prepared dish; top with the marshmallows and ¾ cup sugar.

In a large bowl, using an electric mixer on low speed, cream the lard. Add the remaining 1 cup sugar and the eggs; beat well.

In a separate bowl, combine the flour, salt, and baking powder. Alternately add the flour mixture and the milk to the creamed mixture, beating well after each addition. Pour the batter over the rhubarb mixture in the baking dish.

Bake for 1 hour, until the cake is golden brown. Cool on a wire rack for 5 minutes, then invert the cake onto a serving platter. Cut into squares and serve warm.

SQUASH CAKE

Squash cake is a delightful fall staple when winter squash is fresh and abundant, and we're looking for creative, tasty ways to eat it before storing it for the winter. This simple glaze will give it some zing: Whisk together until smooth ½ cup confectioners' sugar, 2 tablespoons butter, melted, 2 teaspoons lemon juice, and a pinch of lemon zest. Using a spoon, drizzle atop the cake once it has cooled completely. Serves 8 to 10

½ cup lard, softened, plus more for greasing the pan

1¼ cups sugar

2 eggs, well beaten

2¼ cups sifted all-purpose unbleached flour

3 teaspoons baking powder

½ teaspoon salt

½ teaspoon cinnamon

½ teaspoon ginger

½ teaspoon nutmeg

1 cup cooked mashed butternut or acorn squash

¾ cup milk

½ cup chopped pecans

Preheat the oven to 350°F. Generously grease a 9 by 5-inch loaf pan with lard; set aside.

In a large mixing bowl, using an electric mixer on low speed, cream the lard; add the sugar and beat well. Blend in the eggs; set aside.

In a large bowl, sift together the sifted flour, baking powder, salt, cinnamon, ginger, and nutmeg.

In another bowl, combine the squash and milk. Alternately add the flour mixture and the squash mixture to the creamed mixture, beating well after each addition. Fold in the pecans. Pour the batter into the prepared pan.

Bake for 50 minutes, until the cake starts to pull away from the sides of the pan and springs back after being pressed gently with a finger. Cool on a wire rack for 10 minutes, then turn out to cool completely.

Chapter 7

DESSERTS

SWEET POTATO COBBLER

This cobbler is reminiscent of the traditional sweet potato casserole with the toasted marshmallows on top served every year at Thanksgiving—a dish always highly anticipated by all. This version incorporates the marshmallows into the filling and has a flaky, delicious bottom and top crust. Serves 16

CRUST

¾ cup lard, cold and coarsely chopped, plus more for greasing the dish

3 cups plus 3 tablespoons all-purpose unbleached flour

1 teaspoon salt

Ice water

FILLING

4 medium sweet potatoes, washed and peeled

½ cup evaporated milk

3 tablespoons butter

¼ cup granulated sugar

¼ cup brown sugar, packed

½ cup mini marshmallows

1 teaspoon vanilla extract

Pinch of cinnamon

Pinch of nutmeg

1 egg yolk

3 tablespoons water

Homemade whipped cream, for serving

Preheat the oven to 375°F. Grease a 13 by 9-inch baking dish with lard and set aside.

To prepare the crust, in a large bowl, combine 3 cups flour and the salt. Using a pastry blender, cut in the lard until the mixture resembles coarse crumbs. Add just enough ice water to hold together the dough.

Turn the dough onto a floured surface and cut the dough in half. Place one half on floured wax paper and refrigerate. Using a rolling pin, roll out the other half to fit the baking dish. Fit the dough into the bottom of the prepared baking dish, coming up the sides, and bake for 15 minutes (it will be about halfway done); set aside.

Meanwhile, in a medium saucepan over high heat, bring the sweet potatoes to a boil; reduce the heat to medium and cook until tender, about 15 minutes. Remove from the heat but let stand in the cooking water.

Using a slotted spoon, remove the sweet potatoes from the pan and transfer to a cutting board; set aside. To the potato water in the saucepan, add the evaporated milk, butter, the remaining 3 tablespoons (or more) flour, and the sugars (more or less, to taste). Add the marshmallows, vanilla, cinnamon, and nutmeg; blend well. Cook the mixture over medium heat until thickened, whisking often to prevent sticking and to remove lumps. Remove the pan from the heat and set aside.

Slice the sweet potatoes lengthwise and place on the prebaked crust. Dot with additional butter and sprinkle with a little sugar to be sure the filling is sweet enough. Pour the marshmallow mixture over the potatoes. It will be very soupy, but it will cook down.

Remove the reserved dough from the refrigerator and roll out to a ¼-inch-thick rectangle. Cut the dough into strips and place over the filling, crisscrossing the strips. Beat together the egg yolk and water and brush over the top crust.

Bake for 45 to 50 minutes, until the juices have thickened and the crust is golden brown. Cool on a wire rack for 10 minutes before serving. Top with homemade whipped cream.

CHERRY—RHUBARB COBBLER

When driving through the Puyallup Valley in Washington, you'll see acres and acres of rhubarb—with its monstrously large leaves—growing in fields just off the road: not your everyday farm crop. The region grows about 50 percent of the U.S. rhubarb supply. Rhubarb usually is paired with strawberry (and lots of sugar) to tame its tartness, but try this combination for a new take on this beloved vegetable, used as a fruit. **Serves 12**

1 (21-ounce) can cherry pie filling

3 cups chopped fresh rhubarb

2 cups sugar

4 tablespoons butter

½ cup lard

1 egg

1 cup all-purpose unbleached flour

1 teaspoon baking powder

⅛ teaspoon cinnamon

½ cup milk

Preheat the oven to 350°F.

In a large bowl, mix together the pie filling and rhubarb. Spread the mixture in the bottom of a 13 by 9-inch baking dish. Sprinkle with 1 cup sugar and dot with the butter.

Using an electric mixer on low speed, cream together the lard and the remaining 1 cup sugar; add the egg and beat well.

In a small bowl, combine the flour, baking powder, and cinnamon. Alternately add the dry ingredients and the milk to the creamed mixture, beating well after each addition. Pour the mixture over the fruit.

Bake for 50 to 60 minutes, until the juices are bubbling and the crust is puffed and golden brown. Serve warm.

PERFECT PEACH COBBLER

Fresh-from-the-farm peaches are so luscious and juicy, but how do you get those darned fuzzy skins off? For firm peaches, use a sharp vegetable peeler. For very ripe, soft peaches, blanch them in simmering water for 15 seconds, then transfer to a waiting bowl of ice water. The skins should slip off nicely. **Serves 4 to 6**

⅓ cup lard, cold and coarsely chopped, plus more for greasing the dish

3 cups peeled sliced fresh peaches

1 cup plus 3 tablespoons sugar

1 teaspoon grated lemon zest

1 tablespoon fresh lemon juice

¼ teaspoon almond extract

1½ cups sifted all-purpose unbleached flour

2 teaspoons baking powder

½ teaspoon salt

1 egg

½ cup milk

Whipped cream or ice cream, for serving

Preheat the oven to 400°F. Grease a 2-quart round baking dish with lard. Arrange the sliced peaches in the dish.

In a medium bowl, mix together 1 cup sugar, the lemon zest, lemon juice, and almond extract; sprinkle over the peaches. Bake for 10 minutes. Remove from the oven and set aside.

While the peaches are cooking, in a large bowl, sift together the flour, 1 tablespoon sugar, the baking powder, and salt. Using a pastry blender, cut in the lard until the mixture resembles coarse crumbs. In a small bowl, beat the egg and stir in the milk; add this all at once to the lard mixture, mixing just enough to moisten.

Using a large spoon, drop the dough over the cooked peaches, spreading lightly with the back of the spoon. Sprinkle with the remaining 2 tablespoons sugar.

Bake for 30 minutes, until the juices are bubbling and the crust is puffed and golden brown. Serve warm with whipped cream or ice cream.

BANANA BUTTER CRUNCH

If you have a weak spot for sinful breakfast cereals, or even oatmeal slathered with butter, brown sugar, and cream, bookmark this recipe and prepare it next time you're in the mood. Buttery and crunchy, flavored with bananas, oats, brown sugar, and spices, this dish can be served in the morning for brunch or in the evening for dessert. **Serves 6**

⅓ cup lard, cold and coarsely chopped, plus more for greasing the dish

3 cups diced just-ripe bananas (6 to 9 medium bananas)

½ cup granulated sugar

½ teaspoon nutmeg

1 cup brown sugar, packed

1¼ cups sifted all-purpose unbleached flour

1 cup uncooked rolled oats

½ teaspoon salt

½ cup butter, cold, cut into ½-inch cubes

Heavy cream, for serving

Preheat the oven to 375°F. Grease a 2-quart baking dish with lard and set aside.

In a large bowl, combine the bananas, granulated sugar, and nutmeg; toss to coat. Pour into the bottom of the prepared baking dish.

In a large bowl, combine the brown sugar, sifted flour, oats, and salt. Using a pastry blender, cut in the butter and lard until the mixture resembles coarse crumbs. Spread the mixture over the bananas.

Bake for 40 minutes, until the crumb topping is crisp and brown. Cool on a wire rack for 10 minutes before serving warm with heavy cream.

LARD AND POPCORN There is nothing better than popcorn popped in lard. One of our friends, an ag teacher, raised hogs. We went over one night to play cards, and Joe made popcorn. It was completely delicious. When I asked his secret, he said, "I always pop it in lard in a big ol' pan on the stove."

It was well salted, of course, and I just couldn't stay out of it.

Nancy Nemec, West Point, Nebraska

PLUM DUFF

Plum duff is traditionally an English-style pudding—a moist, prune-filled dessert. But this duff is more like a cobbler, with a cakelike crust on top. Dried plums, or prunes, were a popular ingredient in pies in medieval times, but over time they came to be replaced by raisins. The recipes that called for them, however, retained the term "plum," which can be confusing to some cooks. Use stewed plums, prunes, cherries, rhubarb, peaches, apricots, or mixed fruit in this recipe. Serves 6

½ cup lard, cold and coarsely chopped, plus more for greasing the pan

3 cups pitted fresh or canned plums, drained

½ cup plus 1 tablespoon sugar

1 tablespoon butter

1 cup all-purpose unbleached flour

¾ teaspoon salt

1½ teaspoons baking powder

1 egg

¼ cup milk

Warm cream or ice cream, for serving

Preheat the oven to 375°F. Grease an 8-inch square baking dish with lard and arrange the plums in it. Sprinkle with ½ cup sugar and dot with the butter.

In a large bowl, sift together the flour, salt, baking powder, and the remaining 1 tablespoon sugar. Using a pastry blender or two knives, cut in the lard until the mixture resembles coarse crumbs. In a separate bowl, whisk together the egg and milk; stir into the flour mixture and blend well—you'll have a very sticky dough. Spread the dough over the plums.

Bake for 30 to 40 minutes, until puffed and golden brown. Serve immediately with warm cream or ice cream.

EASY COCOA PUDDING

This is in the style of an English pudding—more like a creamy cake than a custard. The boiling water serves to enhance and emphasize the cocoa flavor; it shouldn't be subbed for tepid water. Serve with homemade whipped cream: Beat 1 cup heavy whipping cream with 3 tablespoons sugar on low speed for 30 seconds; add 1 teaspoon vanilla extract and beat on medium-high speed until soft peaks form. **Serves 6 to 8**

1 cup sifted all-purpose unbleached flour

½ teaspoon salt

½ cup sugar

2 tablespoons baking powder

5 tablespoons unsweetened cocoa

¼ cup lard, cold and coarsely chopped

½ cup milk

1 teaspoon vanilla extract

½ cup chopped nuts of your choice

½ cup brown sugar, packed

½ cup light corn syrup

¾ cup boiling water

Homemade whipped cream, for serving

Preheat the oven to 325°F.

In a large bowl, sift together the sifted flour, salt, sugar, baking powder, and 3 tablespoons cocoa. Using a pastry blender, cut in the lard until the mixture resembles fine crumbs. Add the milk, vanilla, and nuts; mix well. Spread the mixture into a 1½-quart casserole dish.

In a medium bowl, combine the brown sugar, the remaining 2 tablespoons cocoa, and the corn syrup; blend thoroughly. Pour in the boiling water and mix carefully until no lumps remain; pour over the mixture in the casserole dish.

Bake for 30 to 40 minutes, until firm on top. Serve warm with homemade whipped cream.

LOTS OF GOOD MEMORIES

My grandmother, mother, and I have all used lard for baking and cooking. I raise heritage hogs and keep the lard for use in everything.

Grandmother's pie crust recipe was never a cup of this and a cup of that. Measurements were stated as "more or less." On Saturday mornings, she would don her baking apron and pull out the enameled washbasins from under the kitchen sink. The kitchen stove was already on, and the kitchen was warming up to a toasty comfort level.

She never had running water in her home; water came from the pitcher pump on the back porch and was heated on the coal stove in the living room in a large galvanized teakettle until she needed it for her pies and bread baking. She would take the 25-pound bag of flour from her pantry and get her lard and hot water to mix the pie dough in the washbasin, adding in a "pinch of salt." She hardly ever used a measuring cup. Baking staples were poured into her basin, and lard was scooped out of the container, usually from a metal lard can, with a spoon.

Every Saturday, Grandma made the favorite 9-inch pie of her five children and their spouses, as well as a few extra pies for Sunday dinner at her house. She also made small individual pies for all nine of her grandchildren. Her children also received some of the best and the most fragrant homemade biscuits, which would measure 6 to 7 inches tall, as well as a loaf of bread. Then, after church on Sunday, all of her children and grandchildren would meet at her home for a dinner of homemade chicken dumplings or homemade beef and noodles made, of course, from lard and flour.

All of Grandma's kitchen towels were made from the flour sacks that the flour came in, and my sister and I would pick up extra ones for her from our local feed store. We would arrive at her door, carrying armloads that the feed store had saved for her.

I have many more memories from my childhood. How about the metal cans that lard came in? Or rendering the fat to make the lard?

When you sit down to an early morning breakfast with home-processed sausage or bacon, pasture-raised eggs, homemade bread, butter, and jelly, homegrown fried potatoes, and milk from your own goats and see the sun come up for another blessed day, you wonder why it took so long to come "back home" and why more people are so slow to start on that path to self-sufficiency.

Vick L. Patton, Hudson, Indiana

APPLE DUMPLINGS

If you want to wow your family and friends with a unique, yet wholly satisfying dessert, prepare these pastry-wrapped apples using organic fruit you picked from the local orchard. Serve warm with cinnamon ice cream for the perfect finish to a fall harvest dinner. **Serves 4**

¾ cup plus 2 tablespoons lard,
cold and coarsely chopped, plus
more for greasing the dish

½ cup plus ⅔ cup sugar

1¾ teaspoons cinnamon

2 tablespoons plus 2 teaspoons butter

1½ cups water

2 cups all-purpose unbleached flour

1 teaspoon salt

Ice water

4 large tart apples (Granny Smith,
Pippin), peeled and cored

Cinnamon ice cream, for serving

Preheat the oven to 375°F. Grease a 13 by 9-inch baking dish with lard; set aside.

In a small bowl, mix together ½ cup sugar and 1½ teaspoons cinnamon; set aside.

In a small saucepan, combine the remaining ⅔ cup sugar, 2 tablespoons butter, the water, and the remaining ¼ teaspoon cinnamon. Heat to boiling and continue to boil gently for 3 minutes. Remove from the heat and set aside.

Sift the flour and salt into a large bowl. Using a pastry blender, cut in the lard until the mixture resembles coarse crumbs. Add just enough ice water (¼ cup, more or less) to hold together the mixture, using your hands to mix. (Don't knead the dough or the pastry will be tough.) Turn the dough onto a lightly floured surface and divide it into 4 balls; roll out each ball and shape into a 9-inch square.

Place 1 whole apple in the center of each pastry square. Fill each apple cavity with the sugar-cinnamon mixture. Using a little water, lightly moisten the edges of each square, then fold the corners up to the center and pinch the edges together. Dot each top with ½ teaspoon butter. Place the apples in the prepared dish. Pour 1 cup of sauce in the bottom of the dish.

Bake for 20 minutes. Remove the dish from the oven and add the remaining sauce; baste. Return to the oven and bake an additional 30 minutes, or until golden brown, basting occasionally. Allow to cool for 10 minutes before serving with cinnamon ice cream.

LOVED THE LEFTOVER CRUNCHIES! I was raised on a farm near Clendenin, West Virginia. I don't remember the recipe, but my brother made pie crust using lard, and they were the best pie crusts I have ever had!

I can remember raising pigs to butcher most of my growing-up years. We butchered them ourselves. We have a family with twelve children, and we raised a lot of what we ate. When I was almost ten years old, I helped Mom with the rendering of fat in a large kettle (a little bigger than a half bushel). We loved the "crunchies" that were left after all the lard was rendered.

I also remember that when we ran out of lard in the kitchen, we bought it in a bucket that was 8 pounds or 25 pounds.

Marshall R. Parker Sr., via e-mail

SAND HILL PLUM DUMPLINGS

Sand Hill plums (Prunus angustifolia) *are native to Kansas. They're found growing wild on dusty prairies, where they're very effective at stopping blowing sand. For native Kansans, that first bite of a ripe Sand Hill plum in July brings with it a flood of childhood memories . . . searching every plum thicket within a five-mile radius for enough fruit for mom to make jelly. If Sand Hill plums aren't available, substitute red plums, but it won't be the same. Serve with a dollop of old-fashioned vanilla ice cream.* **Serves 4**

2½ cups all-purpose unbleached flour

3 teaspoons baking powder

⅓ cup lard, softened

1 cup sugar, plus additional for sweetening

1 egg

⅔ cup milk

1 teaspoon vanilla extract

2 pints Sand Hill plums, washed, pitted, and coarsely chopped

Vanilla ice cream, for serving

In a large bowl, combine the flour and baking powder. In a separate bowl, using an electric mixer on low speed, cream together the lard and sugar; add the egg, milk, and vanilla and beat well. Add the flour mixture to the creamed mixture and beat on low just until combined.

In a saucepan, combine the plums with sugar to taste; heat to boiling and boil for 5 minutes. Using a large spoon, drop the dough into the boiling plums; cover and cook until the dumplings have doubled in size, about 5 minutes. Uncover, remove from the heat, and cool for 15 minutes before serving. The mixture will thicken as it stands. Serve warm with vanilla ice cream.

LONG LINE OF COOKS

I guess I'm probably the last in a long line of lard/bacon grease users. My mom was born and raised in West Virginia, where they raised most of their own food, including hogs, milk cows, and chickens.

I grew up watching my mom cook with rendered lard and/or bacon grease, and that's how I learned to cook. We've always gone to the slaughterhouse to buy our lard. That white stuff in the grocery stores called *lard* just isn't the same as the real thing. The white lard in the grocery stores doesn't have the same rich flavor as lard from the slaughterhouse.

I don't buy as much lard as I used to because I don't cook as much as I used to, and sometimes I do use a little bit of vegetable oil. Sometimes I use oil and bacon grease together to try to make the food more healthy. However, I just can't seem to wrap my brain around the fact that hog fat cooked down into grease is not as healthy as some kind of oil that has been processed and reprocessed with chemicals added.

I've lost faith in the powers that be in telling us what is and what isn't healthy for us, and then five or ten years down the road, they do a complete turnaround.

By the way, my mom lived to be ninety-five years old, eating lard and bacon grease, and I'll soon be seventy-one.

Doris Mathis, northwest Illinois

BROWNIE TORTE DELUXE

This three-layer brownie cake, bursting with marshmallow crème and dripping with chocolate sauce, is just the thing when you're in the mood for celebrating . . . or gluttony. Make it for Mother's Day, when the guest of honor will lovingly nod your way in recognition of your effort.
Serves 16

1½ cups lard, softened, plus more for greasing the pans

3 cups granulated sugar

5 eggs

3½ teaspoons vanilla extract

1 cup plus 2 tablespoons unsweetened cocoa

2¼ cups all-purpose unbleached flour

1½ teaspoons baking powder

½ teaspoon plus ⅛ teaspoon salt

¾ cup butter, softened

2 cups marshmallow crème

2½ cups plus 1⅓ cups confectioners' sugar

3 tablespoons milk

Chopped nuts, for garnish

Maraschino cherries, for garnish

Preheat the oven to 350°F. Grease the bottoms of three 8-inch round cake pans with lard. Cut wax paper to fit the pan bottoms; place in the pans and grease the wax paper with lard. Set aside.

In a large mixing bowl, cream 1 cup lard with the granulated sugar using an electric hand mixer on low speed. Beat in the eggs and 1½ teaspoons vanilla. In a small bowl, sift together 1 cup cocoa, the flour, baking powder, and ½ teaspoon salt. Beat the dry ingredients into the lard mixture.

Divide the batter evenly among the prepared pans and smooth the tops. Bake for 20 to 25 minutes, until the brownie pulls away from the sides of the pan and a toothpick inserted in the center comes out clean. Do not overbake. Remove from the oven; cool on wire racks for 5 minutes. Invert the layers onto wire racks and peel off the wax paper. Cool completely.

In a mixing bowl, cream together ½ cup butter and the remaining ½ cup lard. Add the marshmallow crème and the remaining 2 teaspoons vanilla. Beat well. Add 2½ cups confectioners' sugar and beat until smooth. Set the crème filling aside.

In a small saucepan, heat the remaining ¼ cup butter, the milk, the remaining 2 tablespoons cocoa, and the remaining ⅛ teaspoon salt just until bubbly; stir. Remove from the heat and beat in the remaining 1⅓ cups confectioners' sugar. Set aside to cool. If the glaze becomes too thick while cooling, thin with a tablespoon of milk.

Place 1 brownie layer on a serving plate. Spread a third of the crème filling over the layer. Drizzle a small amount of the glaze over the sides of the layer. Top with a second layer and repeat with the crème filling and glaze. Place the third layer on top. Spread the remaining crème filling over the top and drizzle the remaining glaze over the sides of the torte. Garnish with the chopped nuts and stemmed maraschino cherries.

LARD—WAY OF LIFE

Using lard was a way of life when I was growing up in south Missouri. I was born in 1938. We raised our own hogs, chickens, and milk cows, and we farmed with horsepower. For me, butchering was a hated task, as I detested the smell and the long day of hard work. Mom used the lard and made the best pies, cakes, and yeast bread in the area, according to many people, even those who weren't family. I remember the lard stand in the smokehouse and coming home one Sunday and finding it half empty with someone's handprints in it where they scooped it out.

I used lard in the early days of my marriage, but I gradually came to believe it to be bad for our health. Now, the bad part may be the antibiotics and unhealthy food fed to commercially raised hogs.

Bettie Erwin, Odessa, Missouri

RHUBARB SURPRISE

Rhubarb is the problem fruit of the kitchen. It's extremely tart and always needs its sour nature tamed. This dish uses orange juice and sugar to sweeten rather than the usual strawberries. To further mellow the flavor, before dicing the rhubarb, soak it in a gallon of cold water for 20 minutes. **Serves 6**

⅓ cup lard, softened, plus more for greasing the pan

½ cup plus ⅔ cup sugar

½ cup orange juice

¼ cup water

3 cups diced rhubarb

1 egg

1 teaspoon baking powder

1 cup all-purpose unbleached flour

¼ teaspoon salt

⅔ cup milk

½ teaspoon vanilla extract

Whipped cream or ice cream, for serving

Preheat the oven to 350°F. Grease an 8-inch baking pan with lard; set aside.

In a saucepan, combine the ½ cup sugar, the orange juice, and water. Heat to boiling, add the rhubarb, then reduce the heat to low and simmer for 7 to 10 minutes, until the rhubarb is tender. Stir only once or twice to prevent the rhubarb from becoming mushy. Remove from the heat and set aside to cool slightly.

In a large bowl, cream together the lard and the remaining ⅔ cup sugar with an electric mixer on low speed until fluffy. Beat in the egg, baking powder, flour, and salt. Add the milk and vanilla and beat until well mixed. Pour the batter into the prepared pan and cover with the rhubarb mixture.

Bake for 40 to 45 minutes. Serve warm with whipped cream or ice cream.

APPLE PIZZA

"An apple pie without the cheese is like a kiss without the squeeze," said Park Benjamin Sr., publisher of The Evening Tattler and The New World, in 1882. The traditional way to serve apple pie in England, particularly in Yorkshire and Sussex, is with cheese, which adds a rich, complex flavor. While you probably won't find this apple pizza (with cheddar cheese baked into the crust) served across the pond, it will amuse and delight pizza lovers everywhere. **Serves 8**

CRUST

1½ cups plus ⅓ cup
all-purpose unbleached flour

1¼ teaspoons salt

½ cup lard, cold and coarsely chopped

1 cup shredded cheddar cheese

Ice water

TOPPING

½ cup powdered nondairy creamer

½ cup brown sugar, packed

½ cup granulated sugar

1 teaspoon cinnamon

6 cups apple slices, pared or with peel, sprinkled with 2 tablespoons lemon juice

¼ cup butter, cold

Vanilla bean ice cream, for serving

Preheat the oven to 450°F.

In a large bowl, whisk together 1½ cups flour and 1 teaspoon salt. Using a pastry blender, cut in the lard until the mixture resembles coarse crumbs. Stir in the cheese. Sprinkle the mixture with ice water, 1 tablespoon at a time, and stir until it comes together in a ball. Turn the dough onto a floured surface and roll out to fit a pizza pan (about 15 inches).

To make the topping, in a large bowl, combine the creamer with the sugars, the remaining ⅓ cup flour, the remaining ¼ teaspoon salt, and the cinnamon. Sprinkle a quarter of the mixture over the crust in the pan. Arrange the apple slices in a circular pattern on top.

Using a pastry blender, cut the butter into the remaining sugar mixture until it resembles coarse crumbs; sprinkle over the apples.

Bake for 30 minutes, until the apples are tender and the juices are bubbling. Slice into 8 pieces and serve immediately with a scoop of vanilla bean ice cream.

RESOURCES

Lard

Connecticut Farm Fresh Store: http://www.ctfarmfreshstore.com/product/1435.htm

Fiedler Family Farms: http://www.fiedlerfamilyfarms.com/products.asp

Flying Pigs Farm: http://flyingpigsfarm.com/productdetails.html#serious

Lard Lovers: http://lardlovers.ning.com/

Local Harvest: http://www.localharvest.org/out-until-mar-21%3E%3Eopen-kettle-leaf-lard-C8350

Many Hands Organic Farm: http://mhof.net/meat/index.php

The Meat Shop of Tacoma: http://www.meatshopoftacoma.com/

Old Creek Ranch: http://www.oldcreekranch.net/INDEX.HTML

Prairie Pride Farm: http://prairiepridefarmminnesota.foodoro.com/products/rendered-leaf-lard

Rock House Farm: http://www.rockhousefarm.info/?home,3

Pig Fat

Look under Butcher Shop in the Yellow Pages.

Specialty Spices and Extracts

Atlantic Spice Company: http://www.atlanticspice.com

MySpiceSage: http://www.myspicesage.com

Penzeys: http://www.penzeys.com/

R. L. Schreiber: http://www.rlschreiber.com

Spice Barn: http://www.spicebarn.com

METRIC CONVERSIONS and EQUIVALENTS

Approximate Metric Equivalents

Weight

¼ ounce	7 grams
½ ounce	14 grams
¾ ounce	21 grams
1 ounce	28 grams
1¼ ounces	35 grams
1½ ounces	42.5 grams
1⅔ ounces	45 grams
2 ounces	57 grams
3 ounces	85 grams
4 ounces (¼ pound)	113 grams
5 ounces	142 grams
6 ounces	170 grams
7 ounces	198 grams
8 ounces (½ pound)	227 grams
16 ounces (1 pound)	454 grams
35.25 ounces (2.2 pounds)	1 kilogram

Length

1/16 inch	3 millimeters
¼ inch	6 millimeters
½ inch	1¼ centimeters
1 inch	2½ centimeters
2 inches	5 centimeters
2½ inches	6 centimeters
4 inches	10 centimeters
5 inches	13 centimeters
6 inches	15¼ centimeters
12 inches (1 foot)	30 centimeters

Volume

¼ teaspoon. . . . . 1 milliliter	½ cup (4 fluid ounces) . . . . . 120 milliliters
½ teaspoon. . . . . 2.5 milliliters	⅔ cup . . . . 160 milliliters
¾ teaspoon. . . . . 4 milliliters	¾ cup . . . . 180 milliliters
1 teaspoon . . . . 5 milliliters	1 cup (8 fluid ounces) . . . . . 240 milliliters
1¼ teaspoons . . . . 6 milliliters	1¼ cups. . . . . 300 milliliters
1½ teaspoons. . . . . 7.5 milliliters	1½ cups (12 fluid ounces) . . . 360 milliliters
1¾ teaspoons. . . . . 8.5 milliliters	1⅔ cups. . . . . 400 milliliters
2 teaspoons . . . . 10 milliliters	2 cups (1 pint) . . . . 460 milliliters
1 tablespoon (½ fluid ounce) . . 15 milliliters	3 cups . . . . 700 milliliters
2 tablespoons (1 fluid ounce) . . 30 milliliters	4 cups (1 quart) . . . . .95 liter
¼ cup . . . . 60 milliliters	1 quart plus ¼ cup . . . . 1 liter
⅓ cup . . . . 80 milliliters	4 quarts (1 gallon) . . . . 3.8 liters

Metric Conversion Formulas

To Convert	Multiply
Ounces to grams	Ounces by 28.35
Pounds to kilograms	Pounds by .454
Teaspoons to milliliters	Teaspoons by 4.93
Tablespoons to milliliters	Tablespoons by 14.79
Fluid ounces to milliliters	Fluid ounces by 29.57
Cups to milliliters.	Cups by 236.59
Cups to liters	Cups by .236
Pints to liters	Pints by .473
Quarts to liters	Quarts by .946
Gallons to liters	Gallons by 3.785
Inches to centimeters	Inches by 2.54

Oven Temperatures

To convert Fahrenheit to Celsius, subtract 32 from Fahrenheit, multiply the result by 5, then divide by 9.

Description	Fahrenheit	Celsius	British Gas Mark
Very cool	200°	95°	0
Very cool	225°	110°	¼
Very cool	250°	120°	½
Cool	275°	135°	1
Cool	300°	150°	2
Warm	325°	165°	3
Moderate	350°	175°	4
Moderately hot	375°	190°	5
Fairly hot	400°	200°	6
Hot	425°	220°	7
Very hot	450°	230°	8
Very hot	475°	245°	9

Common Ingredients and Their Approximate Equivalents

1 cup uncooked rice = 225 grams

1 cup all-purpose flour = 140 grams

1 stick butter (4 ounces • ½ cup • 8 tablespoons) = 110 grams

1 cup butter (8 ounces • 2 sticks • 16 tablespoons) = 220 grams

1 cup brown sugar, firmly packed = 225 grams

1 cup granulated sugar = 200 grams

Information compiled from a variety of sources, including *Recipes into Type* by Joan Whitman and Dolores Simon (Newton, MA: Biscuit Books, 2000); *The New Food Lover's Companion* by Sharon Tyler Herbst (Hauppauge, NY: Barron's, 1995); and *Rosemary Brown's Big Kitchen Instruction Book* (Kansas City, MO: Andrews McMeel, 1998).

METRIC CONVERSIONS and EQUIVALENTS

INDEX

NAME

ADDRESS

CITY/STATE/ZIP

EMAIL ADDRESS (REQUIRED)

TGRXXBZ3

Limit one subscription per book purchase.

The order must be accompanied by the original redemption-form page from the cookbook. No photocopies, scans or duplication of any kind will be accepted. Offer open to U.S residents only. If you're already a subscriber, your subscription will be extended. Your first issue mails within six to eight weeks of receipt. We will notify you via e-mail when we've received your redemption form.